In This Issue

PIVOT MAGAZINE

Founder
Jason Miller

President
Juddene Villarin

Web Master
Joel Phillips

Designs
ReliableStaffSolutions.com

Contact

Jason Miller
Founder
1151 Eagle Drive #345
Loveland, CO 80537
jason@strategicadvisorboard.com

Chris O' Byrne
Editor-in-Chief
chris@jetlaunch.net
520-261-3101

From the Editor

This issue of Pivot feels like a masterclass in transformation, delivered by a team of visionaries who have truly walked the path. Each article in these pages offers not only expertise but also a generous dose of heart as our contributors share the strategies and stories that propelled them forward. Together, they form a powerful tapestry of clarity, authenticity, and innovation—a roadmap for navigating the complexities of business today.

As you read, you'll notice a common thread: the courage to embrace change and the wisdom to make it work. Whether it's rethinking how we manage time, approach marketing, or harness the power of technology, these insights challenge us to step beyond the ordinary and into the transformative. The voices in this issue don't just teach; they invite us to rethink, reimagine, and rewrite what success means.

Here's my challenge to you: take these stories and strategies beyond these pages. Use them to spark conversations, fuel decisions, and inspire action. The brilliance of transformation is that it never happens in isolation—it's contagious. Share these ideas with your teams, your partners, and your networks, and watch what grows.

Chris O'Byrne
Editor-in-Chief

From the Desk
Of The President

Building Momentum & Embracing Bold Leadership

As we move into Pivot Magazine's second issue of the year, I can already see the momentum we're building together. In January, I shared my vision for Pivot as a place where entrepreneurs and leaders find clarity, inspiration, and actionable insights. Now, I want to take it even further.

At Pivot, we don't just talk about business—we challenge the way it's done. Every issue is about breaking old patterns, redefining leadership, and finding smarter ways to grow. And that's exactly what this edition delivers.

This month, we're focusing on bold leadership moves, smart strategies, and the power of letting go. You'll find insights from trailblazing entrepreneurs and business minds who have scaled, pivoted, and led with purpose.
To our contributors—your insights continue to shape the conversations that matter.

To our readers—your ambition fuels every page of Pivot. As we move forward together, I want to leave you with a challenge:

- **What's the one leadership shift you can make right now that will create real impact?**
- **Where can you delegate or pivot today to make your business stronger tomorrow?**

Let's make February a month of action. Let's lead, delegate, and scale—together.

JUDDENE VILLARIN *J. V.*

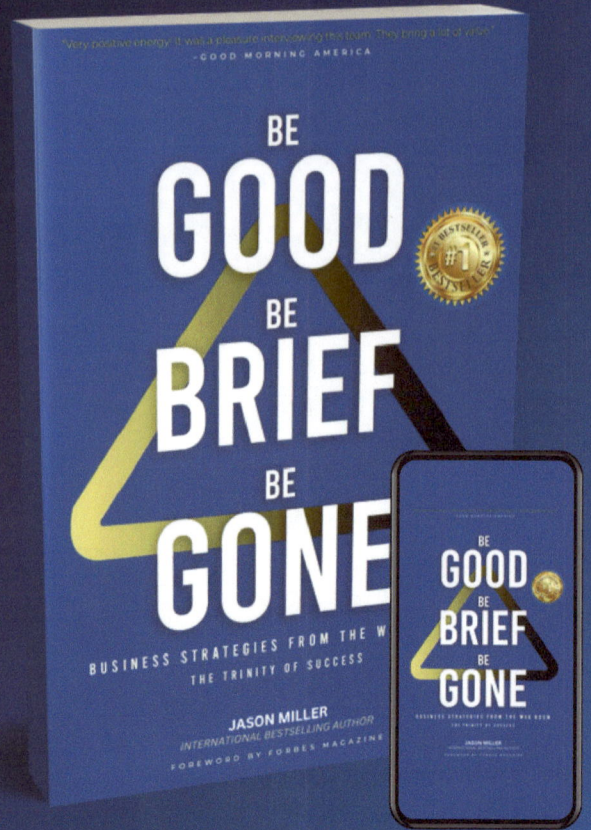

Lead, Delegate, Scale...
The CEO Mindset Shift That Made My Business Thrive Without Me

Juddene Villarin
CEO, Reliable Staff Solutions

~The best leaders aren't the busiest—they're the ones who build teams that thrive without them.

Chris O'Byrne

What pivotal moments in your career forced you to rethink your leadership approach?

Juddene Villarin

I remember working as an executive assistant to a CEO who was drowning in work—handling an overwhelming flood of emails, last-minute payroll issues, customer complaints, and constant fires that needed putting out. She barely had time to strategize because she was consumed by the day-to-day operations, and I saw firsthand how exhaustion was limiting her ability to lead effectively.. At first, I thought that was just part of leadership. But then I started noticing patterns—meetings that could have been emails, tasks she resisted delegating, and opportunities slipping because she was too deep in the weeds.

One day, the CEO was late on a major deliverable because she was buried in admin work. I stepped in, streamlined her schedule, delegated tasks, and created a system for handling non-urgent issues without her involvement. That single shift gave her back 10 hours a week. More importantly, it made me realize that leadership isn't about doing more—it's about enabling others to perform at their best. That was the day I realized— The best leaders aren't the busiest—they are the ones who build teams that thrive without them.

As I refined these delegation systems, executives started noticing. Leaders struggling with similar bottlenecks began reaching out for advice. One of those leaders was Jason Miller, CEO of Strategic Advisor Board and founder of Reliable Staff Solutions (RSS). He saw how I was eliminating inefficiencies and empowering teams, and when he needed someone to lead RSS, he knew I was the right fit. The experience of streamlining operations as an assistant became the foundation for how I scaled RSS into a high-performing, delegation-driven company.

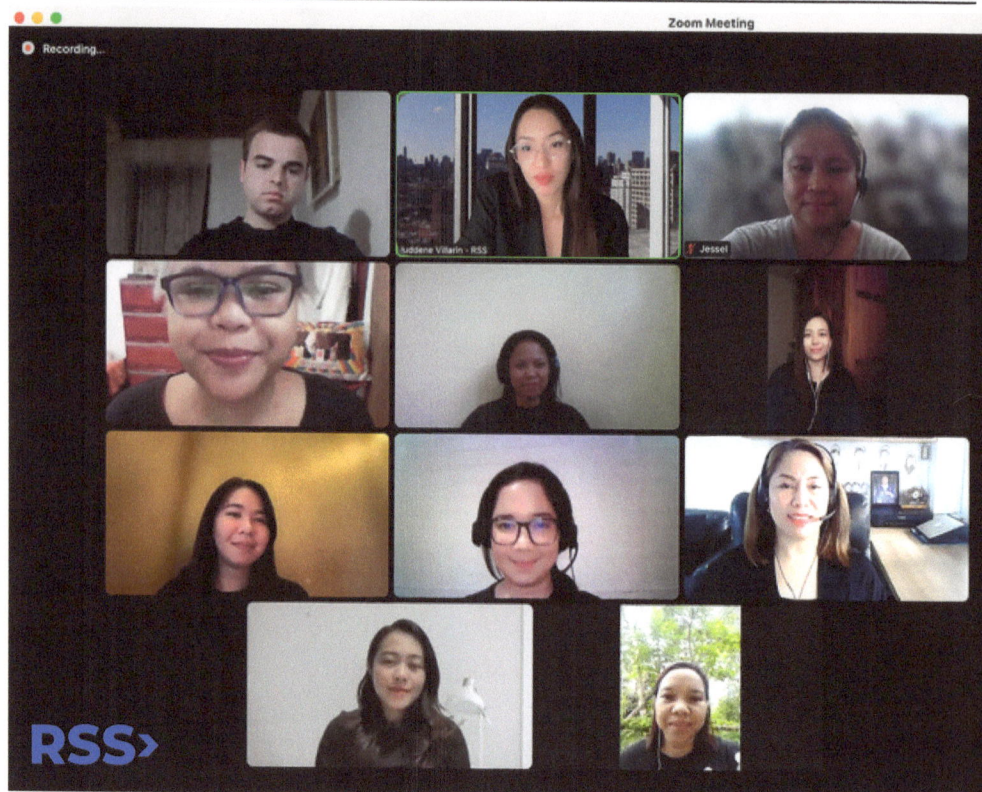

Building Reliable Staff Solutions

Chris O'Byrne

RSS stands out in a crowded market. What was your breakthrough moment in making it unique?

Juddene Villarin

In the early days, we thought the biggest challenge was finding the right people for businesses. But even when we placed top-tier talent, clients were still micromanaging, hesitant to trust their teams. That's when we realized— The real problem wasn't staffing—it was leadership.

So, we made a major shift. We redefined our approach, focusing not just on placing candidates but on educating business owners on trust and delegation. We integrated structured onboarding, team leadership strategies, and performance tracking into our service, ensuring that businesses weren't just hiring— they were evolving into well-run operations with leaders who knew how to let go of control.

We didn't just fill roles—we started coaching leaders on how to delegate effectively, how to build trust with their teams, and how to remove themselves as bottlenecks. The result? Businesses started scaling because they had a team they actually relied on. This transformed RSS from a staffing company into a true business growth partner.

Leading Pivot Magazine

Chris O'Byrne

You now lead Pivot Magazine while running RSS. How do these roles strengthen each other?

Juddene Villarin

RSS helps businesses scale by hiring the right people. But hiring alone isn't enough—you need the right strategies, mindset, and leadership shifts to truly grow. That's where Pivot Magazine comes in.

Many business magazines focus on big success stories, but Pivot is about the real, raw lessons— the hard pivots, the leadership struggles, and the strategies that work in the trenches of business growth.

We don't just talk about scaling;

we break down real-world strategies with actionable insights and case studies that leaders can apply immediately. If you're looking for another magazine filled with billionaire success stories, this isn't it. Pivot is for the business owners in the trenches—figuring out how to grow right now.

Scaling Leadership & Decision-Making

Chris O'Byrne

What's one leadership mistake you've made that changed the way you operate?

Juddene Villarin

I was drowning. Emails, approvals, client escalations—everything ran through me. Then, one day, I looked at my calendar and saw what I had become— a bottleneck in my own business. If I took a day off, everything stalled. That's when I knew—I wasn't running a company. The company was running me.

So, I made a radical shift— I stopped making all the decisions. I empowered my team to own their roles fully, and I implemented systems to make sure decisions didn't always funnel through me. Instead of approving every single project, I gave my leadership team autonomy, and we established clear accountability measures to

track progress without micromanagement. The result? Faster execution, happier employees, and a business that could operate without me constantly being in the middle.

Expanding on Delegation & Leadership

Chris O'Byrne

What's the biggest mindset shift leaders need to truly embrace delegation?

Juddene Villarin

They have to stop seeing themselves as the only problem solver. Many leaders hold onto tasks because they think, "No one can do this as well as I can." But the truth is, someone can— and often, they can do it better when given the trust and responsibility to own the outcome.

Real delegation isn't just about

moving work off your plate; it's about empowering people to step into their expertise. A well-structured team doesn't just wait for orders—they take initiative and solve problems on their own. The best leaders create an environment where their team members feel confident making decisions without second-guessing themselves. it's about building a team that thinks, innovates, and takes ownership. When leaders make that shift, their businesses grow exponentially.

Chris O'Byrne

What's the most underrated skill in leadership today?

Juddene Villarin

Listening. Too many leaders focus on giving direction instead of understanding their team's perspectives.

One of the most game-changing decisions in my business came from listening to a frontline employee. It reminded me that the best ideas often come from the people closest to the work. When you create a culture where your team knows they're truly heard, they'll take initiative, solve problems, and push the company forward— without waiting for you to tell them what to do.

Chris O'Byrne

What's one thing leaders get wrong about delegation?

Juddene Villarin

They think delegation is just about offloading tasks. True delegation is about assigning ownership—not just tasks. When leaders delegate responsibility, not just work, teams feel empowered and make smarter decisions.

If you still have to check everything, you haven't truly delegated.

Chris O'Byrne

How do you balance automation and human leadership in scaling a business?

Juddene Villarin

Automation is a tool, not a replacement for leadership. I believe AI should handle repetitive tasks, so humans can focus on creativity, strategy, and relationships. The best businesses leverage automation to enhance human potential, not replace it.

Chris O'Byrne:

What's one thing leaders get wrong about delegation?

track progress without micromanagement. The result? Faster execution, happier employees, and a business that could operate without me constantly being in the middle.

Expanding on Delegation & Leadership

Chris O'Byrne

What's the biggest mindset shift leaders need to truly embrace delegation?

Juddene Villarin

They have to stop seeing themselves as the only problem solver. Many leaders hold onto tasks because they think, "No one can do this as well as I can." But the truth is, someone can—and often, they can do it better when given the trust and responsibility to own the outcome.

Real delegation isn't just about moving work off your plate; it's about empowering people to step into their expertise. A well-structured team doesn't just wait for orders—they take initiative and solve problems on their own. The best leaders create an environment where their team members feel confident making decisions without second-guessing themselves. it's about building a team that thinks, innovates, and takes ownership. When leaders make that shift, their businesses grow exponentially.

Chris O'Byrne

What's the most underrated skill in leadership today?

Juddene Villarin

Listening. Too many leaders focus on giving direction instead of understanding their team's perspectives.

One of the most game-changing decisions in my business came from listening to a frontline employee. It reminded me that the best ideas often come from the people closest to the work. When you create a culture where your team knows they're truly heard, they'll take initiative, solve problems, and push the company forward—without waiting for you to tell them what to do.

Chris O'Byrne

What's one thing leaders get wrong about delegation?

Juddene Villarin

They think delegation is just about offloading tasks. True delegation is about assigning ownership—not just tasks. When leaders delegate responsibility, not just work, teams feel empowered and make smarter decisions.

If you still have to check everything, you haven't truly delegated.

Chris O'Byrne

How do you balance automation and human leadership in scaling a business?

Juddene Villarin

Automation is a tool, not a replacement for leadership. I believe AI should handle repetitive tasks, so humans can focus on creativity, strategy, and relationships. The best businesses leverage automation to enhance human potential, not replace it.

Chris O'Byrne

What's the best advice you've ever received about leadership?

Juddene Villarin

"If you're the smartest person in the room, you're in the wrong room." Surrounding yourself with people who challenge you is the fastest way to grow as a leader. Never stop learning, never stop evolving.

Chris O'Byrne

If there's one belief that separates successful leaders from struggling ones, what is it?

Juddene Villarin

If your team needs you to function, you don't have a business—you have a job. The real test of leadership? Take a step back for a week. See what happens. If your business thrives, you built something real. If it struggles, you've found the weaknesses you need to fix. Step away for a week. Block off your calendar.

Disconnect. Watch how your business operates in your absence. If your team struggles, you've just identified the gaps in your leadership structure.

If everything runs smoothly, then you know you've built something that can truly scale without you. If your business struggles without you, you know exactly where the weaknesses are. If it thrives, you've built something sustainable. If your business falls apart when you step away, you didn't build a company—you built a cage. And you're stuck inside it.

Scaling Success by Solving Real-World Problems

Alex Kutsishin

> *Entrepreneurship is a journey of bold decisions, strategic action, and continuous learning. Every step shapes the path to success.*

Chris O'Byrne

Because many of our readers are entrepreneurs and focused on growing their businesses, I'd like you to share some of the lessons you've learned. To begin, could you tell us what happened in your life between graduating from high school and starting Fiddlefly?

Alex Kutsishin

After high school, I went to college for two years to play soccer. I attended a community college but left when I could no longer play. After that, I dove straight into business.

At nineteen, I started working in sales for one of my mom's companies. By twenty, I opened my first business—a spin-off of my parents' physical therapy practice. They couldn't open a new location because they were already partnered with another business nearby. In the medical field, you can't compete within a certain distance because people won't travel far for treatment. We lived in Maryland. Washington, D.C., was far enough away to open a new physical therapy practice, so I decided to go for it. I told my parents, "If you're not going to do it, I'll do it. Just show me what we need to do."

Starting the business was an eye-opening experience. Some people grow up fast because they face hardships, like losing a parent or being the responsible one in their family. I grew up fast because I started a business. At nineteen, my weekends began on Thursdays, not Saturdays. However, once I had my own company, I slept in my office in D.C. on Thursdays and Fridays to avoid the long drive in traffic. I went from partying to focusing on my business.

It became an obsession—my healthy obsession. That was my first business. Between then and Fiddlefly, I got involved in many other ventures. We had a printing supply company, a couple of nightclubs, a marketing agency, an apparel company, and even a small software company. We should've stuck with that software company; it later became a successful model in other places.

The marketing agency was the one we really held onto, though. We loved working with fun people and watching companies transform. That led us into the software space, helping software companies build their brands. They began asking if we could help them develop small pieces of software, so we started doing that. Eventually, it became a natural transition to develop our software, and that's where

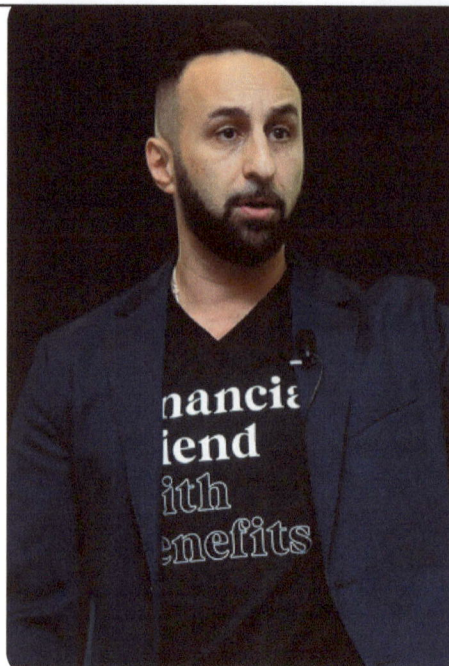

Fiddlefly came from.

You could say I had a strong entrepreneurial upbringing. My parents left Ukraine in 1989 when it was still part of the Soviet Union. It wasn't as simple as packing their bags and catching a flight to New York City. The process took months, traveling through several countries before they finally reached the United States. Within two years of arriving, both had started companies.

What I learned from them wasn't just about being entrepreneurial but about risk tolerance. Entrepreneurs, listen up: The key to success is being willing to take risks. Many people want to start businesses but lack risk tolerance. Starting a business is one of the riskiest things you can do because you're turning an idea that doesn't exist into something real that people will support.

Watching my parents take big risks and succeed taught me that it was okay to take chances. They came out smiling after taking huge risks, which gave me the confidence to do the same. That was my launchpad into entrepreneurship—knowing that if I'm willing to take a risk, even if I fail, I'll be okay. It's a mindset I carry with me in every business venture.

Chris O'Byrne

What was it about the US that made your parents move here?

Alex Kutsishin

I would love to know the answer to that question myself. I don't think I've ever asked my parents why they left. What made them choose the United States? I think their reason for leaving was safety—or rather, the lack of safety in the Soviet Union. As Russian Jews, it wasn't the best place for them to raise a family. So, they took the chance to leave when they had it, seeking the most secure place they could.

My dad grew up with a friend named Alex, whose brother had moved to the United States in the 1970s. When the opportunity came, my dad asked Alex if he would sponsor their move. That's what the Soviet Union required. You couldn't just leave; you had to have someone in the US agree to receive you. That was the only way to leave.

It was a long process, but they came here because someone had already established themselves in the US. There was an apartment waiting for them and a foundation of security. I'm not sure if the idea of the United States influenced their decision, although I assume they'd heard about it while growing up in the Soviet Union. They must have known about life here, especially since they listened to The Eagles—that was their wedding song. They had to know something about the culture, opportunities, and how things were here. However, I'm not sure if the US culture or philosophy made them choose to come here. Either way, taking that risk was worth it.

Chris O'Byrne

Tell me about one of your first companies, Fiddlefly.

Alex Kutsishin

My heart races whenever I talk about Fiddlefly because it was the first company we built at scale. The story behind it is so much fun.

It all began in 2010 when I went to my parents' house for lunch. Their house was just five or maybe ten minutes from our office. I was eating when a commercial came on the TV. At the bottom of the screen was something called a QR code, with a message saying, "For another experience, scan this code and download a QR code scanner."

I thought, "What the heck?" So, I downloaded the QR code scanner while continuing to eat—though I wasn't really eating anymore. I was just waiting for the commercial to come back. I had to experience this thing. It was the end of 2009—not even 2010 yet.

Finally, the commercial returned. I ran to the TV; there was no pausing, by the way. This was before everyone had smart TVs; my parents definitely didn't. I clicked on the code, and to my surprise, a desktop website popped up on my phone. I started zooming in and rotating the screen. I had an old Android Dream phone. Do you remember that one? The one with the flip-out keyboard?

I thought, "What is this?" and immediately felt disappointed. "This is stupid," was my first thought. Then, it hit me: This is a problem that needs solving. Pinching and zooming on a desktop site won't work on mobile. We need mobile experiences—real mobile experiences because a mobile device isn't just a phone anymore; it's your access to the world, and I want that access to be easy.

The next day, I walked into the office and told Serge, an engineer with us at the time. (He's part of our Fuel team now.) I showed him what I had experienced and said, "We need to fix this. Mobile websites need to be mobile experiences." Serge's response was, "That sounds stupid."

I couldn't help but laugh. That's just how he is—direct. However, I knew he was also doing the math in his head, figuring out how to build something to solve the problem.

Two weeks later, after I had been pushing him, Serge came to me with the first version of Fiddlefly. At the time, it was called Web to Mobile (W2M). I looked at it and thought, "This is too technical. We need a brand." So, we decided to change the name to Fiddlefly.

I'll be honest: The first version of Fiddlefly was ugly, but it worked. Serge had scrapped together something that converted a website into a mobile experience. I received an email with a link, opened it on my phone, and clicked on it. The fonts were bigger, and the call button worked. Everything just fit the mobile experience. I was amazed. I didn't even know that was possible.

Just like that, Fiddlefly was born. What followed was an incredible journey. We bootstrapped the company and grew it to have users in over one hundred countries within three years. We never had a single down month. Every month brought more revenue than the last.

Did I sell it? Yes, I sold it to my business partner, James. James is brilliant. He's sold several companies and has a remarkable mind for building and selling business. The sale came when we started to diverge in how we wanted to move the business forward. I had no issues with it; it was a smooth transition. I told him, "You've invested the most, so you have the right to make the decisions now."

James took the company in one direction, and I moved on to start something else.

That time with Fiddlefly was amazing. We shared stages with some of the biggest companies in the world, talking about mobile. We even wrote the book on mobile—literally. Fiddlefly was responsible for shaping how mobile experiences look today.

Think about it: The iPhone came out at the end of 2008 and started gaining popularity in 2009. At that time, nobody was really talking about mobile apps. We started building Fiddlefly at the end of 2009, had a prototype in 2010, and launched it in 2011. When I spoke to people about mobile back then, they'd say, "Yeah, my site works on mobile," but that was it.

We only sold our product to agencies—B2B, not B2C. These agencies had already built hundreds of websites and needed a way to convert them into mobile-friendly sites. With Fiddlefly, they could do that in ten to fifteen minutes. It was fast, simple, and fun.

Chris O'Byrne

Next came Human. Tell me about that company.

Alex Kutsishin

Human came about because I decided to go in a different direction after leaving Fiddlefly and having a baby. The reaction from my wife when I told her what I was planning to do was priceless. She first lost her mind when I told her I was leaving Fiddlefly—lost her mind in a loving way, of course. She asked, "What are you talking about? This is your baby, and you're leaving it?"

Within twenty-four hours, I had started a new company called Agency Human. I said, "Honey, here's my plan. I'm going to start a company called Agency Human because I believe people do business with people, not with companies. My concept is simple: handshakes only, no contracts. Don't do business with me if you don't trust that I will do the job. If you trust that I will, then pay me. I don't need a contract for that; all I need is your word."

My wife responded, "Nobody does business that way in 2014, Alex."

I replied, "We'll find out."

To my surprise, I ended up having many six-figure handshakes. I was generating nearly $300,000 a

year in consulting—all based on handshakes.

So, what did the company do? It was the same thing I've done with all the companies I've built: I helped other companies build their businesses quickly. I'm a big fan of Mario Andretti's mindset —"If you're not scared, you're not going fast enough." That became my motto.

Anyone who wanted to grow quickly came to me. I didn't have time for those who wanted to grow slowly. So, when clients came to me and asked for help, I'd sit down with them and say, "Tell me about your business and how you grow it." After a quick conversation, I would either know exactly how to help them or decide it wasn't a project I was interested in. If it was interesting, we'd always grow their business —every time. We'd use different tactics, but the goal was always the same: growth.

What was the best way to build a business? There is no one-size-fits-all approach. Every business deserves its own path to success. You can take inspiration from other businesses, but for longevity, it must be your way. This is true no matter what industry you're in, whether you're running a coffee shop or a tech company. There's always a reason why one will succeed over another.

So, how did I transition from Human to Sales Boomerang?

My mentor, Ken—who had also been our customer at the marketing agency and wanted to invest in Fiddlefly—became a co-founder at Sales Boomerang. Ken and I had worked together for years, helping him build his brand, which has evolved several times. I re-engaged with his mentorship, telling him I was now a free agent, doing various things. Ken said, "We need you, Alex. We need Agency Human here."

After some discussions, I agreed to join him and started working with his company. Then, something interesting happened. Ken and his team shared a concept with me: a project called Later Leads.

They explained that not every lead generated from marketing converted into a deal for some mortgage companies they worked with. Sometimes, the leads weren't ready because of issues like credit or equity. I mortgage companies they worked with. Sometimes, the leads weren't ready because of issues like credit or equity. I asked, "Okay, so these leads go into a 'later leads' bucket?" They confirmed that was the plan.

I then asked, "What happens to these leads later?" They said they'd follow up with them months later to see if things had changed, like whether their credit score had improved or equity had increased.

I replied, "But how will you know when to follow up with them?" They said they wouldn't; they would follow up every three months.

I paused and said, "I just consulted for a company called Rain King in Bethesda, Maryland. They could predict when Fortune 500 companies needed to replace their technology, which they did with incredible accuracy. That company was acquired for $406 million because of that technology. Are you telling me we can't predict when someone's equity goes up or when their credit improves?"

They asked, "How many people do you think have this problem?"

I responded, "The entire industry."

That's how Sales Boomerang was born. It became the fastest-growing mortgage technology company in the history of mortgage technology, and its technology is now used by virtually every lender in the United States in some form.

Chris O'Byrne

What led you to start Trust Engine?

Alex Kutsishin

Trust Engine came about after we raised money through our firm and completed a transaction in 2021. We acquired a company and merged the two, renaming it Trust Engine. Essentially, it's the same company as Sales Boomerang.

The company is doing beautifully. It's become one of the darlings of the fintech and mortgage technology spaces. I left because I love building new things. It's something I truly enjoy. Then, my phone rang. Todd was on the other end, sharing his vision with me and asking if I could help him bring it to life. I told him how I would approach it if I were in his shoes—and that was when Trust Engine was born.

Chris O'Byrne

How did you meet Todd Duncan?

Alex Kutsishin

One of the most memorable moments of my life was getting a phone call from Todd Duncan, whose audience I had been a part of. When he said, "Hey Alex, this is Todd Duncan," and began explaining who he was, I immediately responded, "I know who you are."

Be a Genius Entrepreneur

Live a life of freedom, optimum performance, and passion.

Genius Entrepreneur group

- ✓ Weekly zoom meetings
- ✓ Community of Support
- ✓ Marketing opportunities

Genius Entrepreneur Program

- ✓ Brand Strategy
- ✓ Signature Program
- ✓ Rogram curriculum

Genius Speaker Series

- ✓ Keynote Speaker training
- ✓ Tedx Training
- ✓ Sell from stage

SHELBY JO LONG
BUSINESS COACHING

Shelbyjolong.com | Business Dynamics

However, when he said, "I've been following your career," I was struck. Those words are engraved in my mind.

He explained that we had been introduced by a mutual connection who thought we should connect, and he wanted to have a call with me. I agreed, and that was it. The conversation immediately felt like a "bro fest;" we clicked instantly. It was as if we had known each other for lifetimes. From that moment, we moved quickly.

I want to dig deeper into Fuel, not only because it's what I'm doing now but also because I believe there are valuable lessons for others in our journey. When Todd and I connected and started discussing ideas, he asked me, "What is your superpower, Alex?" Without thinking, I answered, "Extreme action." That's the key to how we moved from an idea into execution so quickly.

Once something is in motion, there's no stopping it. I've always believed that nothing stands in the way of an idea whose time has come. Once the idea was out there, it had to get moving—and my superpower is extreme action.

I knew how to assemble teams. I've been working with teams since I was twenty-four, and we launched our marketing company at twenty-five. I've always had access to designers, developers, and other experts. Now, I have access to the best in the world—people who work incredibly efficiently and can build products five, six, or even seven times faster than agencies at a fraction of the cost.

We quickly assembled a team and went to work. By May 2022, just a month after our first conversation in April, we had a pilot ready. From there, we moved through alpha and beta testing, launching fully in July 2024. Though we were balancing other commitments at the time, we were fully dedicated to the project.

It was an incredible experience, transitioning from a conversation to a business partnership—a first for me. We moved fast because we both wanted it. Todd has the heart, passion, and experience. He's done this before in the educational space, and I've done it in the technology space. Together, we know how to build teams. It's hard to slow that momentum when you have the desire and ability to make something happen.

Chris O'Byrne

I want the reader to understand how they can also take extreme action.

Alex Kutsishin

First, Todd and I focused on the business model and how we could bring this idea to life. From the start, we understood that the model would evolve. It wouldn't be set in stone, and we knew it could change at any moment. Everyone listening should know this: Don't get too attached to your first approach. It's a huge mistake if you do. If you become overly committed to something and it changes, you'll find yourself stuck, thinking, But we're already committed! If things change, adapt your plan accordingly.

With that in mind, we created a go-to-market strategy. I contacted a few people who could help us design and develop a model. This process took a couple of months. Once we had something, Todd made calls to people he knows, trusts, and loves—people with teams of salespeople he could enlist to test our platform.

One important lesson we learned: no free trials, even if you don't charge them at the end. When people come on for the alpha stage, it has to be a paid alpha, even if they won't be billed. This is crucial. Why? Because free feels different. It has a different value than something you've paid for.

From experience, I can tell you that this is essential.

We built a product with a great customer response during beta when it was free. However, as we prepared for launch, we contacted our beta customers and told them the product would cost money. Suddenly, their enthusiasm waned. They loved it when it was free but were hesitant to pay. This was a key lesson: They need to believe they're paying for something for it to have value in their minds. They'll stick with it once they see the value in what they're paying for.

However, there are exceptions. If you're consulting and don't have a physical product but an intellectual one that creates tangible value, you might consider giving away some of that knowledge for free. This is especially important if your potential clients don't yet understand your offer. Give them a taste of your genius so they can see its value. However, this should never be permanent. It's just a way to demonstrate what you can offer.

The action steps we took were simple: We ensured there was something people would be willing to interact with and pay for, and we gathered their feedback. We quickly received valuable insights. We had our testers on board for about three months, made changes, brought them back for another three or four months, and then launched our beta. The same concept applied: We needed them to agree to pay.

The entire process took about a year. We kept moving forward, sticking to the plan of relentless momentum. The big question was: Could we go live by July? By 2024, we had no product but had gathered all our feedback from the alpha and beta stages. Based on that feedback, we had to make some significant changes. We realized we needed to add video content, something we didn't have at the beginning of the year. By July 8, we launched one hundred video lessons.

How did we manage to create one hundred videos? Todd has a network of people who create great content. He's a publisher with nearly twenty books, so he called friends and shared our vision. We aimed to build a platform focused on positivity and personal development where hard-working individuals could contribute valuable content. We needed instructors passionate about sharing their wisdom, not just making money. They had to be willing to leave a legacy, not just keep their knowledge to themselves.

We were introduced to some of the best instructors thanks to Mac Anderson, our incredible advisor. Within a few months, we had thirty instructors on board, and not long after that, we had

recorded and developed all their content. As for protecting our intellectual property (IP), everything created for Fuel is exclusive to Fuel. The content our instructors contribute can be used elsewhere, but the assets created—like the videos and courses—belong to Fuel. This protects the integrity of our platform. Think of it like Netflix: Netflix content doesn't appear on Prime. Similarly, Fuel's content is exclusive to our platform.

Chris O'Byrne

What do you do to protect your intellectual property?

Alex Kutsishin

Trademarking is incredibly important. Anyone with something valuable should make sure it's trademarked. Regarding copyrighting code, that's something we do regularly. We tend to focus more on copyrighting than patenting. It's a routine part of our process. If anyone tries to steal your code, you can prove it's yours by including special elements in your code—elements only you would know about and that serve a specific purpose.

When protecting software, patenting is important, and I highly recommend it. However, in my career, I've found that winning in the market is the key. To put it simply: Copy all you want. Look at how many pizza shops or car companies exist. There's a market leader in almost every category.

For example, one company stands out when we talk about electric cars. Everyone's got an electric car, but one company is truly winning. It doesn't matter if there are patents or not. Elon Musk has an interesting perspective on this. He famously ripped up his patents and said, "I don't care. Everyone should have access to the best technology." He made his patents available to anyone who wanted to copy Tesla's innovations.

I agree with that mindset. Win in the market. That is your biggest patent. Your go-to-market strategy, approach, service, quality, and results—that's what sets you apart. Sure, if you can patent something—great! But that's a long process. If you're unsure or can't patent something, focus your efforts on winning in the market.

Chris O'Byrne

What should people build into their business model when they're thinking ahead to a potential exit?

Alex Kutsishin

Scalability is an easy answer. If you're building your business with the goal of exiting, scalability is a crucial factor. If you think there's even a chance of an exit, you need to demonstrate your business can scale.

One of the most important things to incorporate into your business—something I've learned as an innovator and visionary—is the need for bulletproof financials. Pay close attention if you're one of those entrepreneurs who typically doesn't focus on this. Your financials must be clear, easy to understand, easy to manage, and easy to explain. If you ever intend to exit, the more straightforward you make this process, the more interest you'll attract and the smoother and faster the process will be.

Make sure you have a strong CFO on your team who can focus on perfecting your numbers. Unfortunately, or fortunately, you're dealing with individuals—often MBAs—who prioritize numbers when they're considering buying your company. They'll likely dismiss it if they have trouble understanding your financials, even if your business is strong. They won't care about your marketing strategies or growth if your numbers don't make sense. Numbers are what drive the decision-making process.

So, make it easy for potential buyers to understand your numbers and ensure they demonstrate how your business will scale. Remember, scalability is key for an exit. However, if your numbers don't align with that potential, it will pose a challenge.

Talent development is a top priority for any leader when preparing for an exit. You must

have a team that is continuously growing and evolving. It's your responsibility to either grow them or let them go. There are two approaches: developing talent up or developing them out.

What does "developing out" mean? Not everyone will remain on your team for the long haul. There are trades, new rosters, and drafts, like in sports. Some people simply can't perform at the required level, and lowering the bar for them affects the entire business.

To maintain a high-performing team, you must constantly raise the bar. Doing so will ensure you have a team that strives to perform because other high performers surround them.

If you're preparing for an exit, the talent on your team is critical. Buyers will want to know who's on your team, how long they've been there, and what you believe about them. These questions will come up. Trust me—if you say, "everyone," they won't believe you. So, be prepared to answer honestly. Who are the key players?

When preparing for an exit, we ensured our leadership team consisted of stars in every position. However, as the company shifted and expectations changed, some of those stars had to move on. Personnel changes are a natural part of the process. The key takeaway is this: If you're heading toward an exit, make sure you're developing your team and cultivating talent.

Chris O'Byrne

As we wrap up our conversation today, I'd like to hear more about Fuel.

Alex Kutsishin

Well, I'm wearing it on my shirt: My Healthy Obsession. What's your healthy obsession? How are you starting today by giving to yourself constantly? How are you inspiring and motivating yourself? You might be doing a lot of things. If you're a habitual learner, a student of life, Fuel is for you. If you're a curious person who believes in sharpening skills that will help you both in your career and personal life, Fuel is for you. If you believe that we, as a world, need more positivity—Fuel is for you.

Fuel is a community built on performance improvement and personal development. There's no such thing as "professional development," so listen closely: Everything is personal development that you can apply professionally. Everything you do is rooted in personal development. You might tell me, "I'm learning how to be an attorney," but you're really learning personal skills—how to communicate, listen, and research. You'll apply those skills in the context of being an attorney, but they're fundamentally personal skills and will be transferable to other fields when the opportunity arises. Fuel is a personal development platform that redefines education. It's no longer about memorization but about applying what you've learned. On Fuel, you instantly apply the concepts you've learned, which helps you retain them 700 percent better than simply listening to or reading something. Memory fades quickly, and details become fuzzy. However, when you practice, it becomes more like muscle memory. That's the difference.

Fuel is a place where you'll hear from some of the most interesting people in the world, all of whom take a heart-forward approach to sharing their lessons. Every lesson has been designed to improve performance—not to help you memorize facts. You're not just learning but building and applying skills on the same day.

For teams, there's Fuel for Teams. This will likely become the number one employee benefit you offer, on top of everything else you provide today. Fuel for Teams offers personal development through binge-worthy content designed to look and feel like the content we all love. It's beautifully done, easy to consume, micro in nature, fun, and exciting. New content is released every week, ensuring nothing gets stagnant. Leaders can track what their teams engage with, which is vital for understanding where employees have gaps in their skills.

The best way to develop talent is to understand where your people need help—not where you think they do but where they know they do. Let me give you an example. When someone on your team watches the "Yes Trap" five times, do you really need to ask them where they need help?

Here's why asking, "What can I help you with?" doesn't work. We built Fuel based on the models of professional sports and the military. Why? Because neither of those environments believes in simply asking people if they need help. Instead, they believe in proving you know how to do something. That's the only way you can be part of the team. I once spoke with Otis, a twenty-six-year Green Beret commander. I asked him if he chose the people on his squad, and he said no. I asked, "Well, how do you become a Green Beret?" He explained that you have to volunteer and undergo a grueling process that 99 percent of people never finish.

Once you're a Green Beret, no one has to remind you of that status. You don't need to keep proving yourself. In sports, does Patrick Mahomes ever think, I should've been an attorney? No. He's exactly where he's meant to be. So why is Fuel for Teams so important? No leader in sports or the military approaches their team members and asks, "What can I help you with?" That's nonsense. Instead, they say, "Here's what you need help with.

I've been thinking about how to help you get better at this." They have a specific plan for developing talent; they're not waiting for the talent to ask for help.

Fuel works the same way. It's designed for you to recognize where people want help. For instance, if someone watches the "Yes Trap" five times, they acknowledge their time management is poor. Now, you meet them where they are and help them with time management—rather than pushing them to work on skills they're not ready for, like closing deals or conversion.

Here's the magic: Fuel is all about autonomy. It's not about forcing people to learn what you want them to learn. It's about letting them choose what's most important to them.

You'll know what they need to work on by watching where they engage. For example, if they choose to watch a course on sales fundamentals, you'll know that time management or conversion skills aren't the issue; they're working on what's important to them.

This approach allows you to identify where someone's strengths and weaknesses lie. You won't know what to develop until they show you. Don't ask them where they need help; let them

demonstrate it through their actions. That's when the real magic happens. So, let your people show you where they need to improve. Support them in that growth, and you'll unlock their true potential. That's the magic.

Action Steps

- Embrace calculated risks in your business decisions: The author emphasizes the importance of risk tolerance as a foundation for entrepreneurial success. Start identifying areas where taking a calculated risk could lead to growth or innovation in your business.

- Focus on scalability from the beginning: To position your business for potential exit or significant growth, ensure your processes, products, and services can scale efficiently as demand increases.

- Invest in developing talent on your team: The author highlights the value of building and nurturing a strong team. Create a culture of continuous improvement by providing training, feedback, and opportunities for personal and professional development.

About the Author

Alex Kutsishin is the co-founder and CEO of FUEL !nc, a groundbreaking performance-as-a-service platform for sales and leadership. A serial entrepreneur with ten ventures to his name, he's pioneered innovations from medical offices to low-code mobile platforms and is an EY Entrepreneur of the Year awardee. Learn more at myfuel.io.

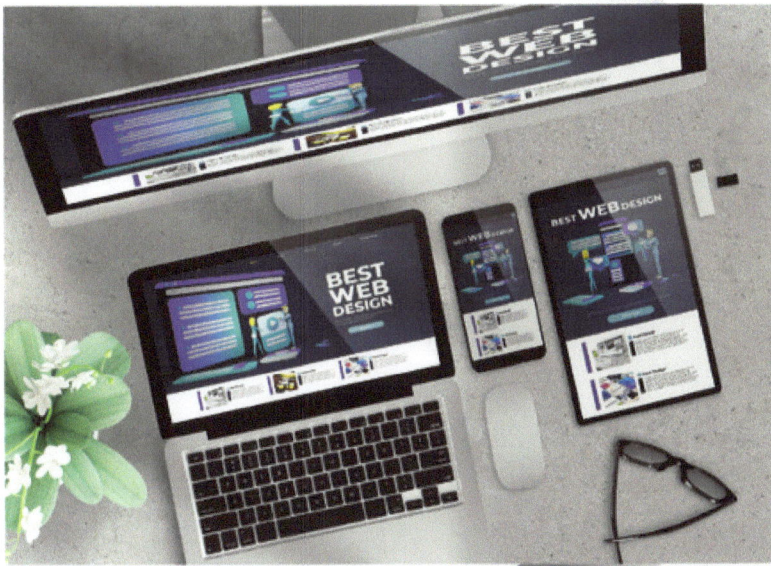

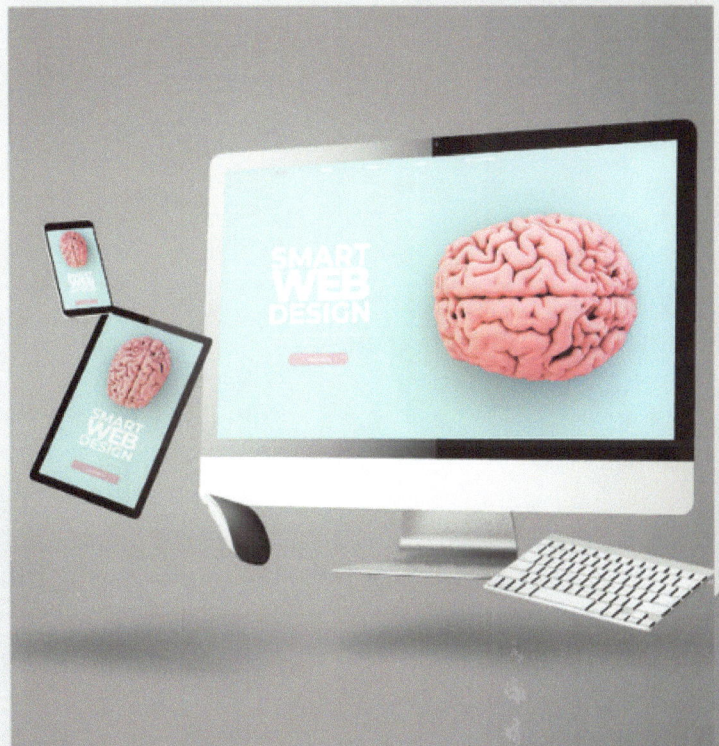

The New Age of Content Marketing: Trends and Predictions

The realm of content marketing is in a constant state of flux, adapting to new technologies and evolving consumer behaviors. 'The New Age of Content Marketing: Trends and Predictions' offers a deep dive into the latest trends that are shaping the way brands connect with their audiences. In today's digital era, where attention is a coveted resource, understanding these trends is critical for any marketer aiming to stand out.

The Rise of Interactive Content

nteractive content is rapidly transforming the landscape of content marketing, offering unique opportunities for audience engagement and data collection. This innovative approach to content creation is reshaping how brands interact with their audiences, turning passive viewers into active participants.

Engaging Audiences with Interactive Experiences

The essence of interactive engage users in a more meaningful way. By incorporating elements that require active participation, such as quizzes, polls, or interactive videos, brands create immersive experiences that capture the audience's attention and encourage deeper interaction. This engagement goes beyond mere viewing, inviting users to become part of the storytelling process and forge a stronger connection with the brand.

Leveraging Technology for Enhanced Interactivity

Advancements in technology are a driving force behind the surge in interactive content. Tools such as augmented reality (AR) and virtual reality (VR) are being utilized to create rich, immersive experiences that were previously impossible. These technologies provide a new dimension to content marketing, allowing brands to offer unique, engaging experiences that stand out in a crowded digital space.

Gaining Insights through User Participation

One of the key benefits of interactive content is the valuable insights it provides into user preferences and behaviors. As users engage with interactive

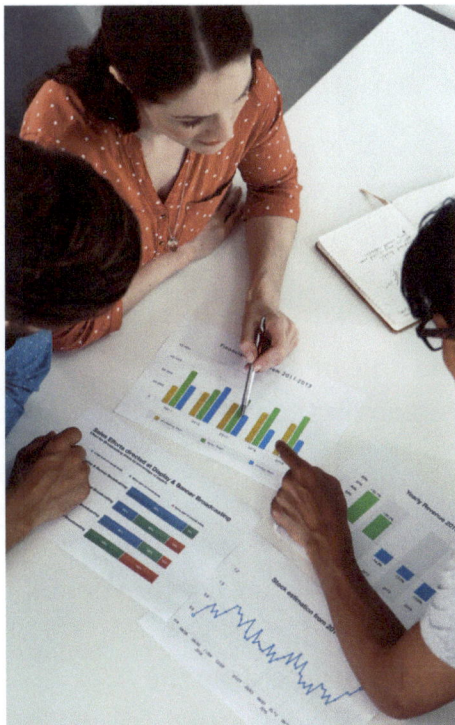

elements, they generate data that offers a wealth of information for marketers. This data can be used to refine marketing strategies, tailor future content, and enhance overall user experience, making content not only more engaging but also more effective in achieving marketing goals.

The Future of Interactive Content in Marketing

Looking ahead, the role of interactive content in marketing is set to grow even further. As audiences become more accustomed to engaging digital experiences, the demand for content that is not only informative but also interactive and entertaining will continue to rise. This shift presents an exciting opportunity for brands to explore new ways of connecting with their audiences and creating memorable content experiences.

Video Content: The New Frontier

In the realm of content marketing, video has rapidly ascended as a dominant and indispensable medium. Its ability to convey messages in a visually engaging and easily digestible format has made it a favorite among audiences and marketers alike, establishing it as the new frontier in digital marketing strategies.

The Growing Influence of Video in Content Marketing

Video content's surge in popularity can be attributed to its versatility and effectiveness in capturing audience attention. From short social media clips to comprehensive instructional videos, the range of content that can be delivered through this medium is vast. Moreover, the

rise of platforms like YouTube, Instagram, and TikTok has further fueled this trend, offering brands new avenues to reach and engage with their target audience.

Innovations in Video Content Creation and Distribution

Technological advancements have significantly lowered the barriers to creating high-quality video content. With the advent of smartphones equipped with advanced cameras and an array of video editing software, creating compelling video content has become more accessible than ever. Additionally, the proliferation of streaming services and video-sharing platforms has provided marketers with numerous channels for distributing their video content, ensuring greater reach and visibility.

Video Content's Role in Driving Engagement and Conversion

Video content has proven to be highly effective in driving user engagement and conversion rates. Its dynamic and immersive nature can convey complex information in an easily understandable manner, making it an ideal tool for tutorials, product demonstrations, and storytelling. This not only helps in building brand awareness but also plays a crucial role in influencing purchasing decisions. In fact, consumers are more likely to buy a product after watching a related video, demonstrating the powerful impact of this medium on consumer behavior.

The Future Outlook for Video Content in Marketing

As we look ahead, the importance of video content in marketing is only expected to grow. Emerging trends like live streaming, 360-degree videos, and interactive video content are opening new possibilities for engaging with audiences. Additionally, the integration of artificial intelligence and virtual reality in video content creation promises to deliver even more personalized and immersive viewing experiences.

Personalization and Customization in Content

In today's digital marketing world, personalization and customization have become key elements in content strategy, setting the stage for more meaningful interactions with audiences. This tailored approach

to content creation and distribution is redefining how businesses connect with their customers, offering a more individualized experience that resonates deeply with their needs and preferences.

Crafting Content that Resonates with Individual Users

The heart of personalization lies in creating content that speaks directly to the individual user. This involves using data and analytics to understand customer preferences, behaviors, and interests, and then tailoring the content to meet these specific needs. Personalized content can range from customized email campaigns to targeted product recommendations on a website. The goal is to make each user feel that the content is specifically designed for them, enhancing engagement and fostering a stronger connection with the brand.

Leveraging Data for Tailored Content Experiences

Data is the cornerstone of effective personalization. By analyzing customer data, businesses can gain insights into what content types and topics are most appealing to different segments of their audience. This information can then be used to create highly targeted and relevant content. Advanced tools like customer relationship management (CRM) systems and data analytics platforms are

instrumental in gathering and interpreting this data to inform content strategies.

The Role of AI in Enhancing Personalization

Artificial Intelligence (AI) and machine learning are playing an increasingly crucial role in content personalization. These technologies enable the automation of content customization, allowing for the scaling of personalized experiences without sacrificing the quality or relevance of the content. AI algorithms can analyze vast amounts of data to predict customer preferences and deliver content that aligns with their interests and behaviors.

The Future of Personalized Content Marketing

Looking forward, the trend of personalization in content marketing is expected to intensify. With advancements in AI and machine learning, along with the increasing availability of data, businesses will be able to deliver even more refined and individualized content experiences. This will not only enhance customer satisfaction but also drive better marketing outcomes, as personalized content typically leads to higher engagement and conversion rates.

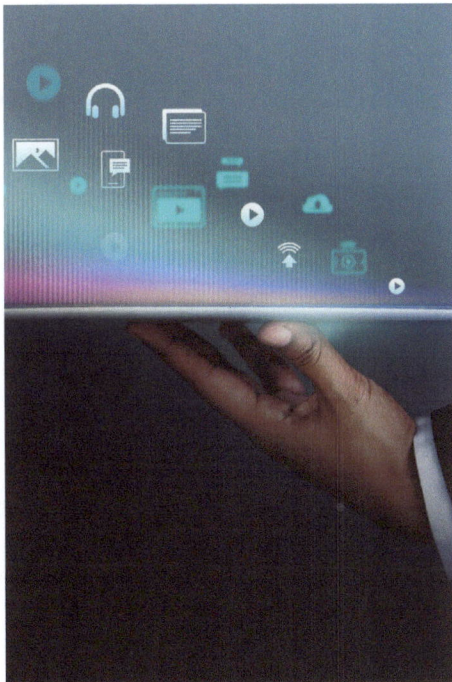

The Growing Relevance of Voice Search in Content Consumption

Voice search is rapidly gaining traction as a preferred method of online searching due to its convenience and efficiency. Users are increasingly turning to searches, find products or services, and even control smart home devices. This shift in search behavior necessitates a change in how content is structured and delivered, with a focus on natural language and conversational tone.

Strategies for Optimizing Content for Voice Search

Optimizing content for voice search involves understanding and adapting to how people naturally speak and ask questions. This includes: Focusing on Long-Tail Keywords: Voice searches are typically more conversational and longer than typed queries. Incorporating long-tail keywords that mimic natural speech patterns can improve the chances of content ranking higher in voice search results.

Creating Content That Answers Questions: Many voice searches are question-based, so content that directly answers specific questions (Who, What, Where, When, Why, and How) can be more effective.
Ensuring Mobile-Friendliness: Since voice searches are often performed on mobile devices, it's crucial that websites are mobile-friendly, with fast loading times and a responsive design.

The Impact of Voice Search on SEO and Content Marketing

Voice search is changing the landscape of SEO and content marketing. Content creators must now consider voice search optimization as part of their SEO strategy to ensure their content remains visible and accessible in this new search paradigm. This includes adapting content to be more conversational, providing clear and concise answers, and optimizing for local search queries, as many voice searches are local in nature.

Future Predictions for Voice Search and Content

As voice recognition technology continues to advance and become more integrated into everyday devices, the impact on content marketing will likely grow. Future trends may include more personalized voice search results based on user history and preferences, and an increase in voice-activated advertisements and content. The integration of voice search data into broader marketing strategies will also become more prevalent, offering new insights into consumer behavior and preferences.

Content Marketing in the Era of Data Privacy

The landscape of content marketing is undergoing a profound transformation in the era of data privacy. With increasing awareness and regulations around data protection, such as the GDPR (General Data Protection Regulation) and CCPA (California Consumer Privacy)

Act), businesses face the challenge of aligning their content marketing strategies with stringent privacy standards while still delivering personalized experiences to their audience.

Navigating Data Privacy in Marketing Strategies

The key to successful content marketing in this new era lies in understanding and respecting the boundaries of data privacy. This involves being transparent about data collection practices and giving consumers control over their personal information. Businesses must ensure that their data collection methods comply with legal requirements and that they maintain the trust of their audience by safeguarding their data.

The shift towards greater data privacy doesn't mean the end of personalized marketing; rather, it signals a move towards more ethical and consumer-centric practices. Marketers can still leverage consumer data, but they must do so in a way that is respectful of privacy concerns.

This could mean relying more on first-party data collected directly from consumers with their consent and using it to create content that is both relevant and respectful of privacy boundaries.

Adapting Content Strategies for Privacy Compliance

Adapting content strategies in the age of data privacy requires creativity and innovation. Marketers may need to explore new ways of gathering consumer insights, such as through direct feedback, social listening, or contextual data analysis, which don't rely on intrusive personal data collection. Additionally, creating high-quality, engaging content that organically attracts audiences can reduce the reliance on personal data for targeting purposes.

The Future of Content Marketing Amidst Privacy Concerns

Looking ahead, the emphasis on data privacy is likely to continue shaping the content marketing landscape. Marketers will need to stay agile, adapting to ongoing changes in privacy regulations and consumer expectations. The businesses that will thrive are those that view these changes not as obstacles, but as opportunities to build deeper trust and more meaningful relationships with their audience through respectful and value-driven content marketing practices.

From the rise of interactive content to the dominance of video, and from the personalized approaches shaped by AI and voice search optimization to the challenges posed by data privacy, the world of content marketing is in constant flux. Businesses that succeed will be those that not only adapt to these changes but also embrace them as opportunities to deepen connections with their audience and deliver more engaging, relevant, and respectful content experiences.

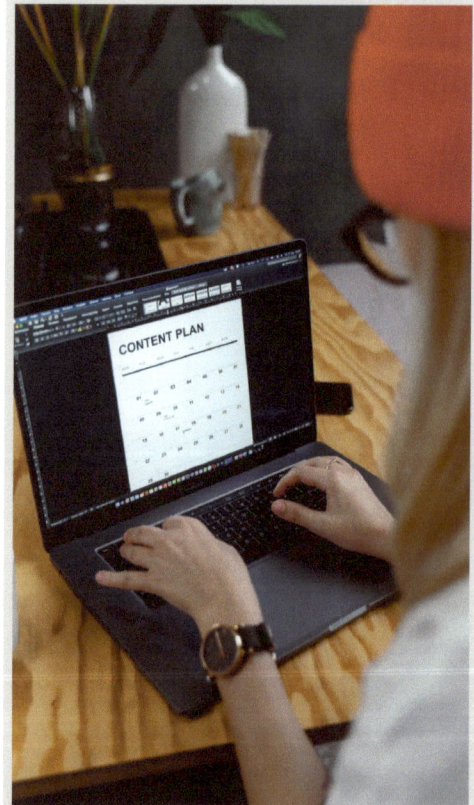

As we move forward, the art of content marketing will increasingly hinge on the ability to balance creativity with technology, personalization with privacy, and innovation with ethical responsibility.

Artificial Intelligence in Sales: A Revolution in Customer Outreach

In a world where competition for customer attention is fierce, businesses are constantly seeking innovative ways to connect, engage, and convert. The adoption of artificial intelligence (AI) in sales represents one of the most profound shifts in modern business practices, heralding a revolution in customer outreach that transcends traditional boundaries.

AI's rise is not accidental; its roots can be traced back to the early days of computer science. However, the advent of machine learning and powerful algorithms has enabled AI's capabilities to flourish in the sales sector. From virtual assistants that converse with potential buyers to predictive analytics that tailor marketing messages, AI's footprint in sales is growing exponentially.

The implications of this technology are far-reaching, reshaping not only how businesses interact with customers but also the very nature of sales and marketing themselves. This article will delve into the technological advancements, the positive impacts, and the challenges that come with the integration of AI into the sales landscape, offering a comprehensive look at a revolution that is changing the way we do business.

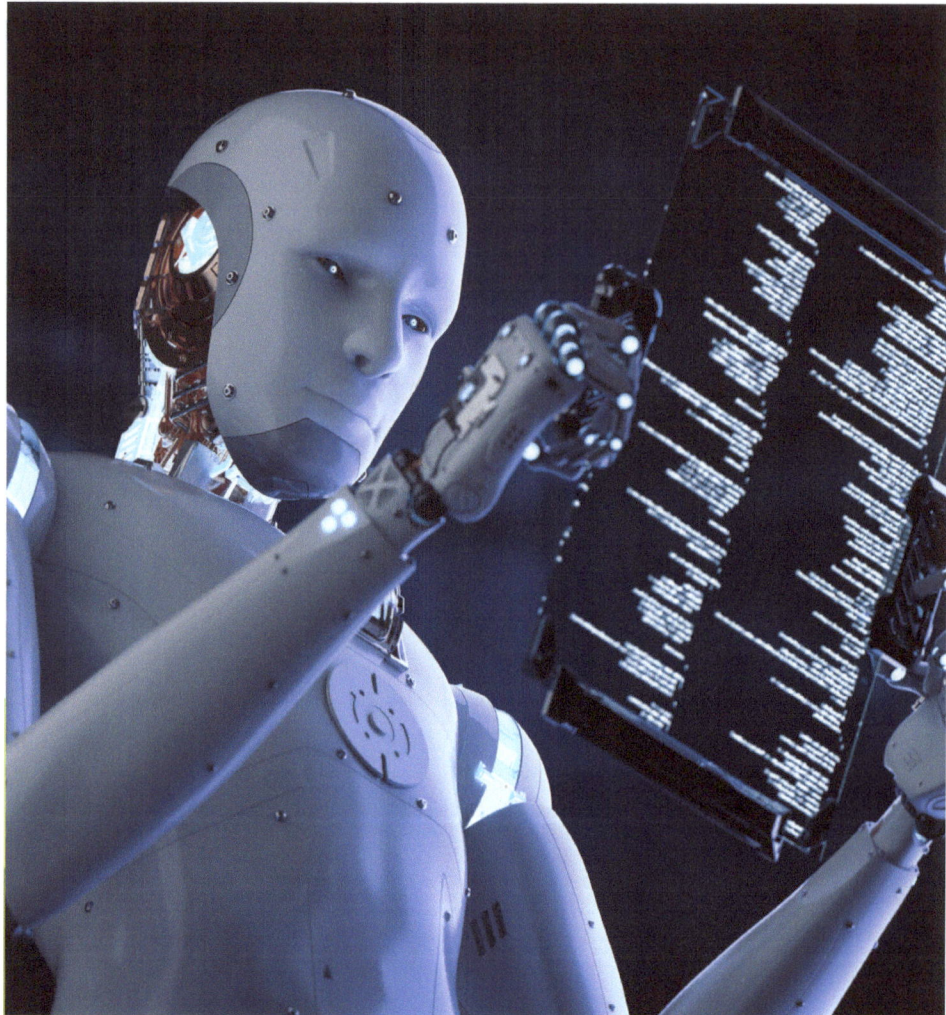

AI Technologies in Sales

The emergence of AI in the sales industry represents a dynamic shift, leveraging advanced technologies to enhance efficiency, accuracy, and personalization. Here's a detailed look at some of the key AI technologies reshaping the sales landscape:

Predictive Analytics

Predictive analytics uses AI algorithms to analyze past data and predict future customer needs and personalize their outreach strategies. This ensures that marketing efforts are targeted, reducing waste and increasing conversion rates.

Chatbots and Virtual Assistants

AI-powered chatbots and virtual assistants are at the forefront of customer service. Capable of handling routine queries and engaging with customers 24/7, these tools offer immediate, consistent support. By employing natural language processing, they can understand and respond to human language, creating more personalized and human-like interactions.

Personalized Marketing

Personalization has become the hallmark of modern marketing. AI enables businesses to analyze vast amounts of data and create unique customer profiles. These insights drive tailored marketing campaigns that resonate with individual preferences and behaviors, thus creating more meaningful connections and boosting sales.

Sales Forecasting

With the ability to process complex data sets and discern underlying trends, AI provides powerful sales forecasting tools. These forecasts assist businesses in planning inventory, allocating resources, and devising targeted sales strategies.

The accuracy of AI-driven forecasting outstrips traditional methods, leading to more informed decisions and efficient operations.

Impact on Customer Relationship Management (CRM)

Customer Relationship Management (CRM) has always been at the heart of successful sales and marketing strategies. With the integration of AI, CRM is experiencing a transformative upgrade, fundamentally altering the way businesses interact with their customers.

Enhanced Customer Engagement

AI enables a more profound understanding of customer behavior and preferences. By analyzing data across various touchpoints, businesses can create more engaging and personalized customer experiences. Whether it's suggesting products based on past purchases or providing proactive customer service,

AI-driven CRM fosters deeper connections and loyalty.

Data-driven Insights

The sheer volume of customer data available can be overwhelming. AI helps by filtering and analyzing this data, transforming it into actionable insights. Sales and marketing teams can now make decisions based on real-time intelligence, leading to more targeted strategies and successful outcomes. It's not about collecting data; it's about understanding it, and AI is the key to unlocking those insights.

Automation of Mundane Tasks

AI can automate numerous routine and time-consuming tasks within the CRM system. From scheduling follow-up emails to updating customer information, automation frees up sales and support teams to focus on more complex and value-added activities. The result is not only an increase in efficiency but also an improvement in employee satisfaction and productivity.

Challenges and Ethical Considerations

While the integration of artificial intelligence in sales brings about revolutionary changes, it also raises certain challenges and ethical considerations that cannot be overlooked. Here are some key areas that demand attention and careful handling:

Data Privacy

AI relies heavily on the collection and analysis of vast amounts of customer data. The management of this data must adhere to privacy laws and regulations. Failure to secure and handle data responsibly not only violates legal standards but also erodes customer trust, potentially leading to significant reputational damage.

Employment Considerations

The automation of various sales processes can lead to concerns about job displacement within the sales and customer support sectors. While AI can handle routine tasks, it's essential to recognize the irreplaceable human elements in sales and foster a collaborative approach where AI complements rather than replaces human roles.

Algorithmic Bias

Algorithms are shaped by the data they are fed, and biases in this data can lead to biased outcomes. Whether it's unintentional reinforcement of stereotypes or unequal treatment of different customer segments, algorithmic bias can create ethical dilemmas and even legal challenges. Continuous monitoring and adjustment of AI systems are vital to ensure fair and unbiased operations.

Dependency on Technology

Overreliance on AI systems may create vulnerabilities, especially if technical malfunctions occur. Balancing the use of technology with human oversight ensures that businesses can continue to operate effectively even if technological challenges arise. Furthermore, dependency on AI without critical thinking and human judgement may lead to suboptimal business decisions.

Implementation Strategies: A Guided Approach to Embracing AI in Sales

The exciting potential of AI in sales is clear, but translating this potential into tangible results requires a guided approach to implementation. Here's a roadmap to help businesses successfully integrate AI into their sales strategies:

Assessment and Planning

Before diving into AI integration, organizations must assess their specific needs,

capabilities, and goals. This involves understanding current processes, identifying areas for improvement, and defining clear objectives for AI adoption. A well-thought-out plan will act as a blueprint for success.

Choosing the Right Tools and Platforms

Selecting the right AI tools and platforms is essential to align with business needs. Whether it's chatbots for customer service or predictive analytics for marketing, carefully considering functionality, scalability, and compatibility with existing systems ensures a seamless transition.

Training and Development

Implementing AI requires investment in training and development. This includes educating the sales and support teams on how to use AI tools effectively and possibly hiring or developing in-house expertise to manage and optimize the systems.

Monitoring and Optimization

AI's effectiveness is not set in stone; continuous monitoring and optimization are vital. Regularly evaluating the performance of AI tools, gathering feedback from both customers and staff, and making necessary adjustments will keep the systems aligned with evolving business needs and market trends.

Ethical Considerations and Compliance

The responsible use of AI must remain at the forefront of implementation. Adhering to data privacy laws, considering the impact on employment, and actively working to avoid algorithmic biases are essential to build trust and ensure legal compliance.

Measuring AI's Impact on Sales Performance.

Embracing AI in sales isn't simply about implementing new technologies; it's about understanding and quantifying the value these technologies bring to an organization.

Defining Key Performance Indicators (KPIs)

Setting clear and relevant KPIs is essential to measure success.

These could include metrics like increased conversion rates, reduced customer service response times, or improved sales forecasting accuracy. KPIs should align with the specific objectives that guided the AI implementation.

Continuous Monitoring and Analysis

Monitoring the performance of AI tools continuously allows organizations to track progress and detect any areas that may need adjustment. Analysis of data over time can reveal trends and insights that directly translate into actionable improvements.

Customer Feedback and Satisfaction

Customer feedback is a crucial metric for evaluating AI effectiveness in sales. Collecting and analyzing feedback on customer interactions with AI-powered tools can provide insights into how well these technologies meet customer needs and expectations.

Cost-Benefit Analysis

Calculating the ROI of AI in sales requires a comprehensive cost-benefit analysis. This involves measuring the total investment in AI (including costs for technology, training, and maintenance) against the tangible and intangible benefits gained, such as increased sales, enhanced customer loyalty, or more efficient operations.

Ethical and Compliance Auditing

Ensuring that AI practices align with ethical guidelines and regulatory compliance is an integral part of evaluation. Regular auditing of AI systems to confirm adherence to privacy laws and ethical standards fosters trust and protects the organization's reputation.

Future Trends and Opportunities

The integration of AI into sales is just the beginning of a continually evolving landscape. As technology advances and businesses adapt, new trends and opportunities are emerging that promise to further redefine the way organizations engage with customers. Here's a look at some of the exciting developments on the horizon:

Continued Innovation

Innovation in AI is accelerating, leading to more sophisticated and nuanced tools. Whether it's improving the empathy of chatbots or enhancing predictive analytics' accuracy, continuous innovation will drive more effective and engaging sales strategies.

Integration with Other Technologies

AI does not exist in a vacuum; its power can be magnified through integration with other emerging technologies such as the Internet of Things (IoT), blockchain, and augmented reality (AR). These synergies can lead to more immersive customer experiences and new avenues for engagement.

New Markets and Opportunities

As AI becomes more accessible and affordable, opportunities for its application in various markets and industries will grow. Small and medium-sized businesses will benefit from AI-driven tools that were previously out of reach, democratizing access to advanced sales technologies.

Ethical AI Development

With growing awareness of the ethical considerations surrounding AI, there is a trend towards more responsible and transparent AI development. This will likely lead to standardized guidelines and best practices, aligning AI implementation with societal values and legal requirements.

Personalized Customer Journeys

The future of sales lies in providing uniquely tailored customer journeys. AI enables a level of personalization that is beyond manual capabilities, allowing businesses to create individualized paths that guide customers from discovery to purchase, fostering loyalty and satisfaction.

Artificial Intelligence in sales isn't just a passing trend. It's a transformative shift redefining how businesses connect with customers. From predictive analytics and personalized marketing to its game-changing impact on Customer Relationship Management (CRM), AI has reshaped the very foundation of sales strategies. Businesses are leveraging AI-driven insights to anticipate customer needs, streamline operations, and drive smarter decision-making. By automating repetitive tasks such as data entry, lead scoring, and customer follow-ups, AI allows sales teams to focus on what they do best: building relationships and closing deals.

However, this evolution comes with its share of challenges. The integration of AI into sales demands significant investment, both in terms of financial resources and training. Many businesses struggle with the complexity of AI adoption, from selecting the right tools to ensuring seamless implementation. Additionally, ethical concerns surrounding data privacy and AI-driven decision-making must be addressed.

Transparency, responsible data usage, and compliance with regulations such as GDPR are crucial to maintaining customer trust. Companies that navigate these challenges effectively will be better positioned to harness AI's full potential.

Despite these hurdles, the future of AI in sales brims with innovation, promising to elevate customer engagement to unprecedented levels. Conversational AI, chatbots, and virtual assistants are already transforming how businesses interact with prospects, offering real-time support and tailored recommendations. AI-driven sentiment analysis helps sales teams gauge customer emotions, allowing for more personalized and effective communication. As AI continues to evolve, advancements in machine learning and natural language processing will further refine how businesses understand and respond to customer needs.

Embracing AI in sales isn't merely about adopting new technology; it's about adapting to a dynamic, customer-centric approach that aligns with ever-evolving expectations.

Businesses that remain resistant to AI risk falling behind as competitors leverage data-driven insights to refine their strategies and enhance customer experiences. The revolution is here, and for companies ready to seize the moment, the road ahead is rich with promise, potential, and progress. Those who embrace AI's capabilities today will not only drive growth but also set the standard for the future of sales.

The Complete Guide to Scale Up Your Company

When scaling up a company, there is no one-size-fits-all approach. Every business is different, and each has its unique set of challenges and opportunities for growth. That said, some basic principles apply to all businesses looking to scale up.

What Do You Mean By Scaling?

Scaling up a company means growing the business in a sustainable and profitable way. It generally involves expanding into new markets, increasing sales and marketing efforts, and adding new products or services. It can also involve expanding your physical infrastructure, such as opening new offices or warehouses.

The goal of scaling up is to increase revenue and profits while also ensuring that the company can continue to operate effectively as it grows. It can be challenging, as many businesses find that their existing systems and processes cannot cope with rapid growth.

To scale up successfully, businesses need to understand their customers and what they want clearly. They also need a robust sales and marketing strategy and the ability to adapt and change as the market evolves.

How To Scale Your Business?

There is no single formula for success when scaling a business. However, there are some key principles that all businesses should follow.

Evaluate Your Strengths

The statistics show that only 44% of small businesses survive their first four years. It is unsurprising because 80 percent do not make it to year two in business!

There are several reasons for this, but one of the key factors is that many businesses do not clearly understand their strengths and weaknesses.

Before you can scale your business, you need to take a step back and evaluate what you do well and where there is room for improvement. It will help you identify the areas where you need to focus your energies to succeed.

Define Your Target Market

One of the most important things you need to do when scaling a business is to define your target market. It might seem like a no-brainer, but many businesses make the mistake of trying to be everything to everyone.

This is not only impossible but also a surefire recipe for failure. When trying to appeal to everyone, you end up appealing to no one.

The key to success is to focus your efforts on a specific target market. It could be a certain geographical area, a particular demographic, or even a specific niche.

By clearly defining your target market, you can tailor your sales and marketing efforts to appeal directly to them. It will make it much easier to generate leads and convert sales.

Create A Sales And Marketing Plan

Once you have defined your target market, you need to create a sales and marketing plan to help you reach them. This plan should include a mix of online and offline tactics, such as search engine optimization (SEO), content marketing, social media marketing, email marketing, and traditional advertising.

It is important to track your progress and measure the results of your sales and marketing activities. It will help you fine-tune your strategy and use the most effective tactics.

Invest In Technology And Promote Innovation

Technology can be a powerful tool for scaling a business. The right technology can help you automate processes, stay organized, and improve communication.

When choosing technology for your business, investing in products that will scale with you is important. It means choosing products that are flexible and can be customized to meet your changing needs.

In addition to investing in technology, it is important to promote innovation within your team. Encourage your employees to develop new ideas and ways to improve the business.

Note that innovation and creativity are not the same things!

Focus On Your Customer Experience

The customer experience should be at the heart of everything you do when scaling a business.

It means creating a seamless customer journey from start to finish.

Every touchpoint with a customer should be positive and memorable. It includes everything from the initial contact to post-purchase follow-up.

You must ensure that your employees are trained to deliver the best customer experience. It will help ensure that your customers keep returning, even as you scale.

Remember, it costs 6-7 times more to acquire a new customer than to keep an existing one!

Get Finances In Order

Scaling a business can be an expensive endeavor. You need to ensure that you have the finances in order before starting.

It means having enough cash to cover unexpected costs, such as repairs or unanticipated expenses. It is also important to have a line of credit or another financial safety net in case of slow periods.

In addition to having the financial resources in place, you also need to ensure that your accounting and bookkeeping are up to date. It will help you to keep track of your expenses and ensure that you are making sound financial decisions. You may be able to grow your business without any investment if you're lucky,

without any investment if you're lucky, but the amount of cash needed for scaling will vary depending on demand and how much success there has been in bringing new customers. If it's not enough already, consider hiring more employees or investing in marketing tools that can help increase revenue—but keep an eye out because things might change drastically later down this road!

Focus On Efficiency

Scaling a business can be chaotic and hectic. It is important to focus on efficiency to keep things running smoothly.

It means streamlining processes, automating tasks, and eliminating anything that does not add value. The goal is to make your business as lean and efficient as possible.

It will help you to save time and money as you scale

It plays a big role, especially in the early stages when resources are limited, and you're still trying to find your footing.

Evaluate Your Business Infrastructure And Tools

As your business grows, it is important to re-evaluate your infrastructure and tools. It includes everything from your website to your customer relationship management (CRM) system.

You will need to update your infrastructure to accommodate your growing business as you scale. It may mean upgrading your website, switching to a new CRM system, or adding new tools to your toolkit.

Don't be afraid to make changes to your infrastructure as you grow. The goal is to have a robust and scalable infrastructure to support your business as it expands.

In a successfully scaled business, each piece of your infrastructure should work together to enable you to do the best possible job for customers.

For example, operational tools help employees perform their tasks efficiently and effectively, which allows them to take care of all aspects, from receiving final payment up until closing out an account or providing customer service over email inquiries quickly, so there's less turnaround time spent waiting on hold with vendors back home base!

The more scalable we are as entrepreneurs-the happier our investors will be too!

Keep An Eye On Your Competitors

Scaling a business can be a competitive process. As you scale, you must keep an eye on your competitors.
It means understanding their strengths, weaknesses, and strategies for growth.

You can use this information to adapt and improve your strategies.
It is also important to stay up to date on industry trends. It will help you to identify new growth

opportunities.Remember, the goal is to scale your business in a way that allows you to stay ahead of your competitors.

Stay Lean And Make Your Customers Happy

As you scale your business, it is important to stay lean. It means eliminating anything that does not add value.It is also important to keep your customers happy. It means providing them with the best possible experience. The goal is to create a scalable

business that is efficient and provides an excellent customer experience.
Scaling a business isn't always easy, especially when you're starting out.

But one way to make it easier is by staying leaner than your competition (and remember: More isn't always better). It all comes down to doing work with less-- keeping costs low while still delivering high-quality products or services for customers who keep coming back time after time!

What is the difference between scaling and growing in your business?

The main difference between scaling and growing a business is that scaling refers to increasing the size or capacity of your business while growing refers to increasing the revenue or profit of your business.

Scaling is often necessary to accommodate a growing business, but it is not always sufficient. You may need to grow your business to generate more revenue.

Growing a business is often difficult because it requires finding new customers or selling more products to existing customers. Scaling a business is often easier because it requires you to increase the size or capacity of your business. However, both are scaling and growing a business can be challenging.

What Should You Scale In A Business?

Scaling a business is an exciting yet challenging endeavor that requires careful planning and execution. As a business grows, there are key areas that need to be scaled effectively to ensure long-term success. Below are the most crucial aspects to focus on when scaling your business.

Employees

Hiring the right employees is essential for scaling a business successfully. As demand for your products or services increases, your workforce needs to grow accordingly. However, it's not just about hiring more people. It's about hiring the right people. Look for employees who are passionate about your company's mission, have the necessary skills, and are willing to contribute to its growth.

Once you have the right team in place, it's equally important to keep them engaged and motivated. Offering flexible work schedules, ongoing training, and career development opportunities will not only retain top talent but also prepare them for new challenges as the company expands. Engaged employees are more productive, creative, and committed, which ultimately leads to greater business success.

Systems and Processes

As your team grows, so does the complexity of your business operations. Without well-defined systems and processes, rapid growth can lead to inefficiencies, miscommunication, and operational bottlenecks. Establishing clear workflows, automating repetitive tasks, and implementing technology-driven solutions will help streamline operations and maintain consistency as your business scales.

Having structured processes in place ensures that employees can work efficiently and stay aligned with the company's goals. This is especially important when dealing with an increasing number of customers, orders, and responsibilities. Whether it's customer service, inventory management, or financial reporting, scalable systems help prevent chaos and ensure smooth day-to-day operations.

Customer Experience & Financial Management

Scaling a business requires maintaining high-quality customer service while handling increased demand. Investing in customer support, refining sales processes, and using CRM systems or chatbots can enhance customer interactions and ensure long-term satisfaction.

Financial stability is also crucial for growth. Effective budgeting, forecasting, and cost control help prevent cash flow issues. Tracking key financial metrics and securing funding through investors or loans can support expansion without overextending resources.

Scaling a business involves more than just increasing revenue; it requires a strategic focus on key areas such as employees, systems, customer experience, and financial management. Hiring the right team, implementing efficient processes, and leveraging technology can help businesses operate smoothly as they grow. Ensuring that employees remain engaged and well-trained is essential for maintaining productivity and meeting rising demands.

Additionally, prioritizing customer experience and sound financial management is crucial for sustainable growth. Businesses must invest in customer support, refine their sales processes, and use data-driven insights to maintain strong relationships with their audience. At the same time, careful financial planning, through budgeting, forecasting, and securing necessary funding, ensures stability and prevents cash flow challenges, allowing for long-term success.

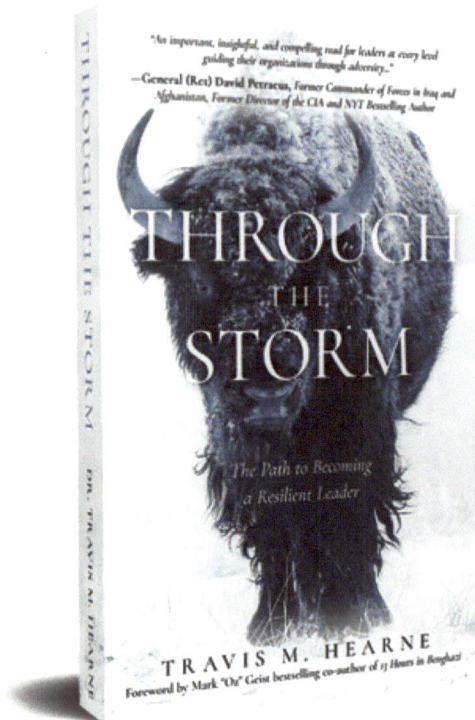

Enhancing Legal Services: Integrating AI for Improved Case Analysis and Client Management

In the swiftly evolving legal sector, staying ahead means embracing innovation, particularly in technology. Artificial Intelligence (AI) is at the forefront of this transformation, offering groundbreaking solutions for case analysis and client management. This integration promises not only to streamline workflows but also to enhance the quality of legal services. As you embark on reading this article, you will discover how AI is revolutionizing the legal field, from conducting thorough legal research to managing complex client relationships effectively. Embrace this journey into the future of legal practice, where AI stands as a pivotal tool in redefining efficiency and precision.

The Emergence of AI in the Legal Field

The legal industry, traditionally known for its adherence to precedent and time-honored practices, is currently undergoing a significant transformation with the emergence of Artificial Intelligence (AI). This shift is driven by the need for greater efficiency, accuracy, and client service in an increasingly complex legal landscape. AI in the legal field is not just a AI in the legal field is not just a futuristic concept; it is a present reality altering the very fabric of legal practices.

AI's initial foray into the legal world was met with skepticism. However, its potential for transforming vast amounts of legal data into actionable insights quickly turned AI into an invaluable asset. Legal professionals began to see AI's capability in performing tasks ranging from document review to legal research, tasks that once consumed considerable time and resources.

One of the most notable applications of AI in law is in the realm of predictive analytics. AI systems can analyze legal precedents and outcomes of past cases to predict future results with remarkable accuracy. This ability not only aids lawyers in crafting more effective legal strategies but also helps in assessing the risks and benefits of different legal actions.

One of the most notable applications of AI in law is in the realm of predictive analytics. AI systems can analyze legal precedents and outcomes of past cases to predict future results with remarkable accuracy. This ability not only aids lawyers in crafting more effective legal strategies but also helps in assessing the risks and benefits of different legal actions.

Another significant impact of AI in the legal field is the automation of routine tasks. AI-powered tools are capable of sifting through thousands of documents in a fraction of the time it would take a human, identifying relevant case laws, and even drafting basic legal documents. This automation not only speeds up the legal process but also frees up attorneys to focus on more complex and strategic aspects of their work.

Moreover, AI is reshaping client-lawyer interactions. AI-driven chatbots and virtual assistants are now capable of providing initial legal consultation, guiding clients through legal processes, and answering routine inquiries. This not only enhances client service but also allows lawyers to allocate their time more efficiently.

Despite these advancements, the integration of AI in the legal field is not without challenges. Concerns regarding the ethical implications of AI decision making, data privacy, and the

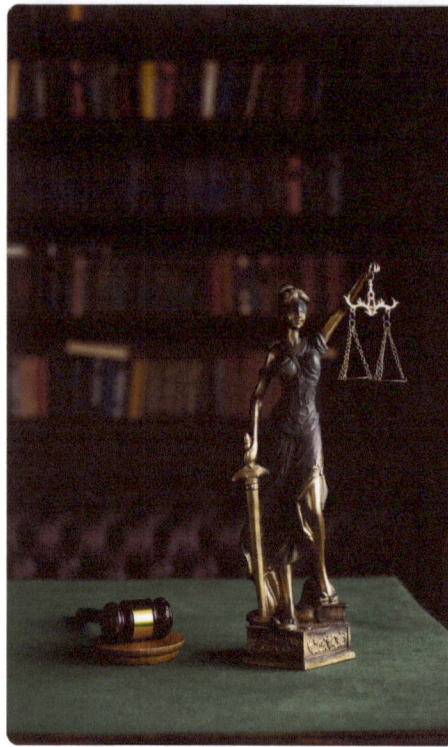

potential for job displacement in the legal sector are subjects of ongoing debate.

AI in Legal Research

AI's impact on legal research is reshaping how legal professionals approach their investigative work. Traditionally, legal research has been a time-intensive task, requiring meticulous sifting through volumes of case law, statutes, and legal literature. AI has revolutionized this process by enabling faster and more accurate research, transforming how legal professionals gather and analyze information.

Modern AI systems in legal research use advanced algorithms to scan through vast legal databases. They can identify relevant case laws, statutes, and legal precedents in a fraction of the time it would

take a human researcher. This efficiency is not just about speed; it also enhances the thoroughness of the research. AI tools can uncover hidden connections and insights that might be missed in manual research due to the sheer volume of data.

Moreover, AI in legal research is not limited to mere keyword matching. These systems are increasingly sophisticated, capable of understanding context and nuances in legal texts. They employ natural language processing to interpret the meaning of words and phrases, providing more relevant and accurate results. This capability is particularly beneficial in complex legal

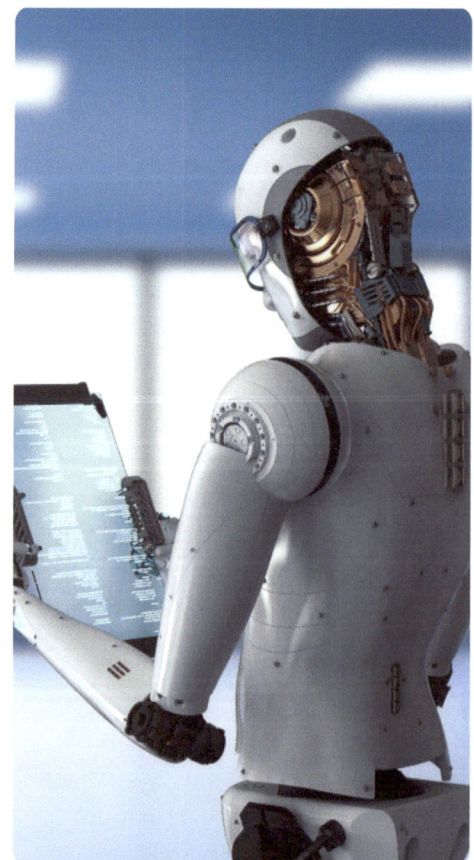

research tasks where the context and subtleties of legal language play a crucial role.

AI also contributes to predictive legal analysis. By analyzing past legal decisions and trends, AI tools can predict potential outcomes of cases, offering valuable insights for lawyers as they develop legal strategies. This predictive capability enables lawyers to advise clients more effectively and make informed decisions about how to proceed with cases.

Another significant benefit of AI in legal research is its accessibility. Cloud-based AI legal research tools have democratized access to legal information, allowing smaller firms and independent practitioners to access the same wealth of resources as larger firms. This shift levels the playing field in the legal industry, promoting a more equitable access to legal resources.

Despite these advancements, the integration of AI in legal research also presents challenges. It requires lawyers to have a certain level of technical proficiency to utilize these tools effectively. Additionally, there's an ongoing need to ensure that AI systems are unbiased and ethical, particularly when it comes to interpreting laws and legal precedents.

Enhancing Client Management with AI

The integration of AI into client management in the legal sector represents a significant leap forward in how law firms and legal professionals interact with and serve their clients. AI technologies are redefining traditional client management approaches, making them more efficient, personalized, and responsive.

One of the major advantages of AI in client management is the automation of routine communication and administrative tasks. AI-powered chatbots and virtual assistants can handle initial client inquiries, schedule appointments, and provide clients with basic information about legal processes. This not only improves the efficiency of client service but also allows legal professionals to focus on more complex aspects of their cases.

Personalization is another area where AI is making a substantial impact. AI algorithms can analyze a client's history and preferences to provide tailored advice and services. This level of personalization enhances the client experience, as it demonstrates a deeper understanding of their individual needs and circumstances.

Moreover, AI tools aid in client data management by organizing and analyzing vast amounts of data. They can track communication history, case details, and client preferences, enabling lawyers to access relevant information quickly.

This efficient data management leads to better-informed decisions and strategies, ultimately benefiting client outcomes.

AI also plays a critical role in client risk assessment. By analyzing past cases and outcomes, AI can help lawyers identify potential risks and advise clients accordingly. This predictive capability ensures that clients are better prepared for various legal scenarios, enhancing trust and confidence in the legal services provided.

However, incorporating AI into client management is not without its challenges. Ensuring the security and confidentiality

of client data is paramount, as is maintaining the personal touch that is crucial in lawyer-client relationships. Balancing the efficiency of AI with the need for human empathy and understanding remains a key consideration.

AI in Document Review and Management

The application of AI in document review and management is revolutionizing how legal documents are handled within the legal industry. This change is marked by increased efficiency, accuracy, and a significant reduction in the time and resources traditionally required for document-related tasks.

In the realm of document review, AI brings a level of speed and precision that is unattainable through manual processes. Utilizing machine learning algorithms, AI systems can quickly sift through thousands of pages of documents, identifying relevant information, categorizing documents, and even highlighting potential issues. This capability is particularly valuable in cases involving large volumes of discovery materials or complex contractual agreements.

Another aspect where AI excels is in pattern recognition and anomaly detection. The technology can identify inconsistencies and irregularities in documents that might escape human reviewers. In the legal context, this means AI can flag clauses in contracts that deviate from standard language or identify missing elements in legal documentation, thus mitigating risks and ensuring compliance.

AI also contributes to better document management. By organizing and indexing documents, AI systems make it easier for legal professionals to retrieve information. These systems can tag documents with relevant keywords, cross-reference related materials, and even suggest related documents based on the content being reviewed. This level of organization streamlines workflow and enhances overall productivity.

Moreover, AI-driven document management systems facilitate collaboration among legal teams. With features like version control and real-time updates, team members can work on documents simultaneously, ensuring consistency and efficiency. This collaborative aspect is especially important in legal settings where multiple professionals need to review and contribute to the same documents.

The introduction of AI in document review and management is not without challenges. One of the primary concerns is ensuring that AI systems are properly trained to understand the nuances of legal language and the specific requirements of different legal documents. There is also the need to maintain a balance

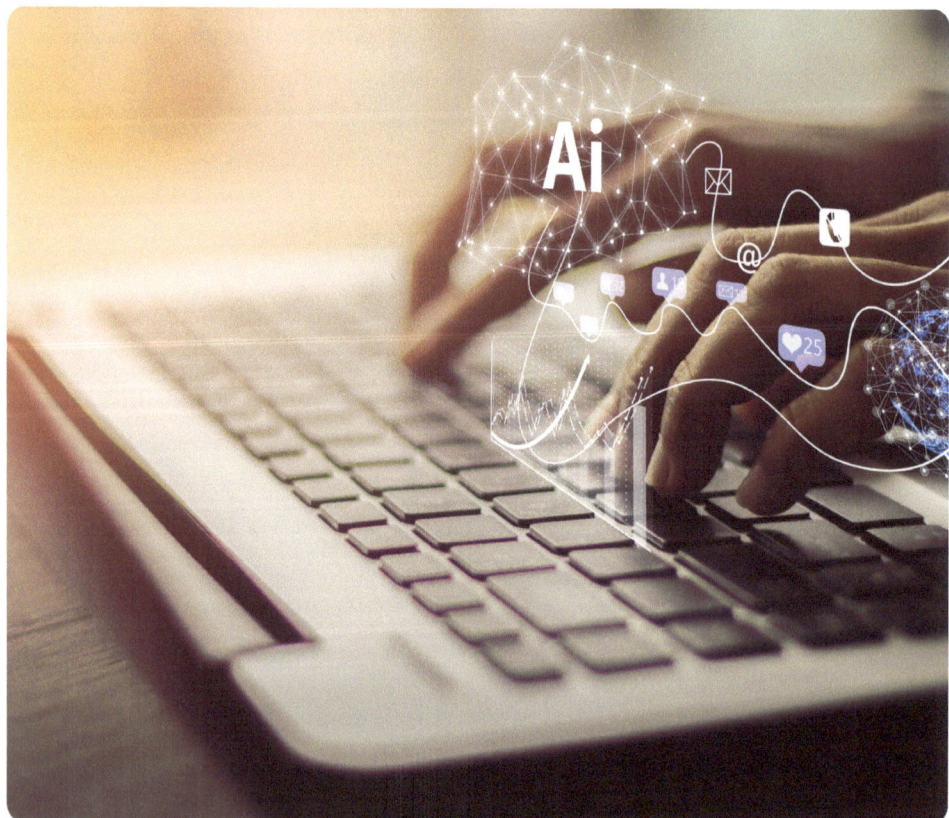

between automated and human review to ensure accuracy and to address the ethical implications of automated decision-making.

Ethical Considerations and Data Privacy

As AI continues to integrate into various aspects of legal practice, it brings forth a range of ethical considerations and data privacy concerns that must be addressed. The legal profession, bound by strict ethical codes and a commitment to client confidentiality, faces unique challenges in ensuring that AI tools adhere to these same high standards.

One of the primary ethical concerns is the transparency and accountability of AI systems.

Given that AI algorithms can be complex and not always easily interpretable, there's a risk of opaque decision-making processes. It's crucial for legal professionals to understand how AI tools arrive at conclusions and ensure that these processes are transparent and justifiable. This understanding is necessary to maintain trust with clients and uphold the integrity of the legal process.

Data privacy is another critical issue in the realm of AI in law. Legal practices handle sensitive client information, and ensuring the security and confidentiality of this data is paramount. As AI systems require access to vast amounts of data to function effectively, it's vital to implement robust security measures to protect against data breaches. Additionally, compliance with data protection regulations, such

as the General Data Protection Regulation (GDPR), is essential.

The potential for bias in AI systems also raises ethical concerns. AI tools are only as unbiased as the data they are trained on, and if this data reflects existing biases, the AI's decisions could be skewed. Legal professionals must be vigilant in ensuring that AI tools are trained on diverse, unbiased data sets and are regularly reviewed for potential biases.

Moreover, the increasing reliance on AI in legal processes prompts questions about the diminishing role of human judgment. While AI can significantly enhance efficiency and accuracy, the unique insights and ethical reasoning provided by human professionals remain indispensable. Balancing the use of AI with the critical thinking and ethical judgment of legal practitioners is necessary to ensure the responsible use of technology.

The Future of AI in Legal Services

The future of AI in legal services is poised to further transform the industry in profound ways. As AI technology continues to evolve, its potential applications within the legal field are vast and varied. This future trajectory is not only about enhancing current practices but also about reimagining what legal services can be.

One of the most exciting prospects is the development of more advanced AI systems capable of handling increasingly complex legal tasks. These systems might be able to conduct more nuanced legal research, provide sophisticated legal advice, and even assist in strategizing for cases. As AI becomes more adept at understanding and interpreting legal language and concepts, its role as a decision-support tool will become more significant.

The integration of AI in legal services is also likely to lead to more predictive legal analytics. AI could be used to forecast legal trends, predict the outcomes of cases, and identify potential legal issues before they arise. This predictive capability would enable lawyers to be more proactive, offering clients strategic advice that anticipates future legal landscapes.

Another area where AI is expected to make significant strides is in customization and client service. AI could enable highly personalized legal services, where client interactions and legal solutions are tailored to individual client needs and preferences. This level of personalization would enhance client satisfaction and engagement.

The future also holds potential for greater collaboration between AI and human legal professionals. Rather than viewing AI as a replacement for human lawyers, the focus will likely shift to how AI can augment human capabilities. This collaborative approach would leverage the strengths of both AI and human intelligence, leading to more efficient and effective legal services.

However, the future of AI in legal services will also need to address the challenges of ethical considerations, data privacy, and the need for regulatory frameworks. As AI becomes more ingrained in legal practices, the legal profession will need to develop new guidelines and standards to govern the use of AI, ensuring that it is used responsibly and ethically.

AI is poised to revolutionize the legal industry, enhancing case analysis, automating document review, and improving client management. These advancements allow legal professionals to work faster and more accurately while optimizing workflows, reducing costs, and improving service delivery. This transformation benefits both practitioners and clients by making legal services more accessible, affordable, and personalized.

However, as AI reshapes the legal landscape, it's crucial to balance innovation with ethical and regulatory concerns, such as data privacy, algorithmic bias, and the need for human oversight. Legal professionals must ensure AI complements rather than replaces human expertise by adopting responsible AI practices and clear ethical guidelines. With thoughtful implementation, AI can drive a future where legal services are not only more efficient but also more precise, fair, and client-focused.

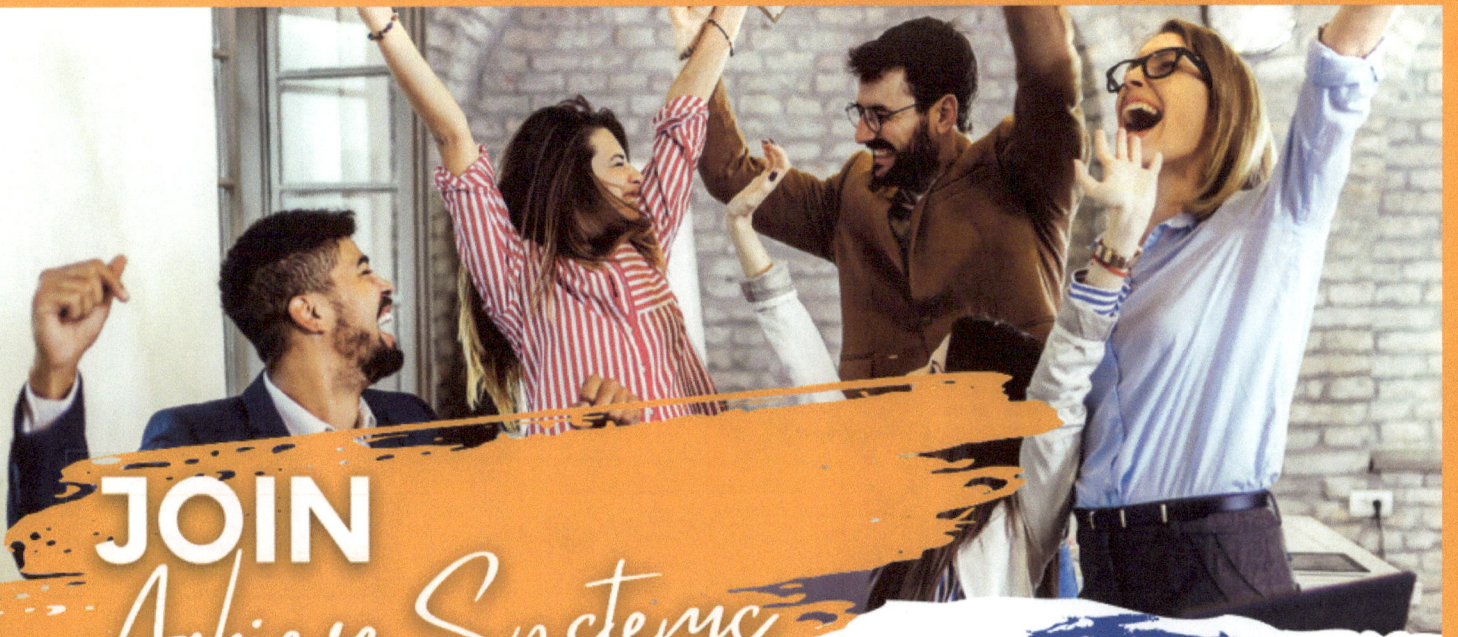

JOIN
Achieve Systems

BECOME AN ACHIEVE SYSTEMS MEMBER TODAY!

Education

We help you get the tools to create a thriving business! It's turnkey, you can start NOW!

Marketing

We provide marketing guidelines but also plug you into our conferences, events and database

Community

We have a thriving community of entrepreneurs and business owners for you to collaborate, refer and partner with to grow and up-level your business!

WE WORK WITH ENTREPRENEURS, BUSINESS OWNERS, SPEAKERS & LEADERS!

CONTACT US OR REGISTER HERE: www.AchieveSystemsPro.com

6 Steps To Improve Your Company's Culture And Allow It To Reach Its Full Potential

Company culture is a crucial aspect of any business, impacting employee morale, customer satisfaction, and ultimately, the bottom line. If your company culture is not up to par, it can hold your business back and prevent it from reaching its full potential. In this article, we will outline 6 steps you can take to improve your company culture and allow it to reach its full potential. From defining your company values and communicating them to your employees, to fostering a positive work environment and recognizing the hard work of your team, these steps will help you create a strong and **healthy company** culture that can drive success.

What is culture, and why is it important?

Culture refers to the shared beliefs, values, customs, behaviours, and practices that characterize a group or organization. It is the unique identity of a company, and it shapes the way that employees interact with each other and with customers.

Culture is important because it can have a significant impact on the success of a business.

A positive company culture can lead to increased employee morale and retention, higher customer satisfaction, and ultimately, greater success for the business. On the other hand, negative company culture can lead to low employee morale, high turnover, and poor customer satisfaction.

Company culture is key to reaching the full potential

A strong company culture is essential for a business to reach its full potential. It sets the tone for the way that employees interact with each other and with customers, and it can have a significant impact on the success of the business.

By focusing on building a positive company culture, businesses can create a supportive and inclusive environment that encourages collaboration and innovation. This, in turn, can lead to increased employee morale and retention, higher customer satisfaction, and ultimately, greater success for the business.

On the other hand, a negative company culture can hold a business back and prevent it from reaching its full potential. It can lead to low employee morale, high turnover, and poor customer satisfaction, all of which can hinder the growth and success of the business.

In conclusion, company culture is key to reaching the full potential of a business. By focusing on building a positive and supportive culture, businesses can create an environment that encourages

6 Steps To Improve Your Company's Culture

As a business owner or manager, you know that company culture is crucial to the success of your business. It affects everything from employee morale and retention to customer satisfaction and the bottom line. If your company culture is not up to par, it can hold your business back and prevent it from reaching its full potential.

So, how do you go about improving your company culture and allowing it to reach its full potential?

1. Define your company culture

Defining your company culture is an important step in the process of improving your company culture and allowing it to reach its full potential. Your company culture is the unique identity of your business, and it shapes the way that employees interact with each other and with customers. By defining your company culture, you can establish the values and behaviors that are important to your business and ensure that they are reflected in all aspects of your company culture.

Here are some steps you can take to define your company culture:

Identify your core values: What are the values that are most important to your business? These values should be reflected in all aspects of your company culture.

Communicate your values: Make sure that all employees understand your company values and how they should be reflected in their work.

Hire for fit: When hiring new employees, make sure they align with your company values and will fit in with your company culture.

Establish company-wide policies and procedures: Establish policies and procedures that reflect your company values and support a positive company culture.

Lead by example: As a leader, it's important to model the values and behaviours you want to see in your company culture.

By defining your company culture, you can establish a clear set of values and behaviours that will shape the way that employees interact with each other and with customers. This, in turn, can help improve your company culture and allow it to reach its full potential.

2. Promote a positive work environment

Promoting a positive work environment is an important step in the process of improving your company culture and allowing it to reach its full potential. A positive work environment can have a significant impact on employee morale and productivity, and it can ultimately contribute to the success of your business.

Here are some steps you can take to promote a positive work environment:

Create a welcoming and inclusive atmosphere: Make sure that your workplace is welcoming and inclusive, and that all employees feel valued and supported.

Foster a culture of respect: Create a culture of respect by promoting open and honest communication, and by treating all employees with kindness and respect.

Encourage work-life balance: Encourage work-life balance by offering flexible work arrangements and promoting a healthy work-life balance for all employees.

Provide resources for employee well-being: Offer resources such as employee assistance programs and wellness programs to support the well-being of your employees.

Recognize and reward hard work: Recognize and reward the hard work and contributions of your employees. This can help motivate and engage employees and foster a positive work environment.

By promoting a positive work environment, you can create a supportive and inclusive atmosphere that encourages collaboration, innovation, and success. This, in turn, can help improve your company culture and allow it to reach its full potential.

3. Encourage creativity and innovation

Encouraging creativity and innovation is an important step in the process of improving your company culture and allowing it to reach its full potential.

Creativity and innovation can help your business stay competitive and drive growth, and a culture that encourages these qualities can foster a sense of innovation and collaboration among employees.

Here are some steps you can take to encourage creativity and innovation in your company culture:

Foster a culture of continuous learning: Encourage employees to learn and grow professionally by providing opportunities for professional development and training.

Encourage employees to share their ideas: Encourage employees to share their ideas and suggestions for improvement. This can help foster a sense of ownership and encourage innovation.

Encourage risk-taking: Encourage employees to take risks and try new things. This can help foster a culture of innovation and drive growth.

Create a supportive and inclusive environment: Create a supportive and inclusive environment that encourages collaboration and innovation.

Recognize and reward creative ideas: Recognize and reward creative ideas and contributions. This can help motivate and engage employees and encourage creativity and innovation. By encouraging creativity and innovation, you can create a culture that fosters collaboration and drives growth. This, in turn, can help improve your company culture and allow it to reach its full potential.

4. Celebrate team successes

Celebrating team successes is an important step in the process of improving your company culture and allowing it to reach its full potential. By recognizing the hard work and achievements of your employees, you can foster a sense of accomplishment and pride in the work that they do. This, in turn, can help motivate and engage employees and contribute to a positive company culture.

Here are some steps you can take to celebrate team successes:

Recognize and reward team achievements: Recognize and reward the achievements of your teams. This can be in the form of verbal recognition, written recognition, or rewards such as gift cards or team outings.

Share team successes with the company: Share the achievements of your teams with the rest of the company. This can help foster a sense of pride and accomplishment among all employees.

Celebrate team successes publicly: Consider celebrating team successes publicly, such as through social media or in company-wide meetings. This can help build morale and encourage a sense of pride in the company. Take the time to celebrate: Make sure to take the time to celebrate team successes and show your appreciation for the hard work and achievements of your employees.

By celebrating team successes, you can foster a positive company culture and motivate and engage your employees. This, in turn, can help improve your company culture and allow it to reach its full potential.

5. Recognize individual contributions

Recognizing individual contributions is an important step in the process of improving your company culture and allowing it to reach its full potential. By acknowledging the hard work and achievements of your employees, you can foster a sense of accomplishment and pride in the work that they do. This, in turn, can help motivate and engage employees and contribute to a positive company culture.

Here are some steps you can take to recognize individual contributions:

Provide regular feedback: Provide regular feedback to your employees to let them know how they are doing and to recognize their contributions.

Recognize and reward individual achievements: Recognize and reward the achievements of your employees. This can be in the form of verbal recognition, written recognition, or rewards such as gift cards or individual outings.

Share individual achievements with the company: Share the achievements of your employees with the rest of the company. This can help foster a sense of pride and accomplishment among all employees.

Recognize individual contributions publicly: Consider recognizing individual contributions publicly, such as through social media or in company-wide meetings. This can help build morale and encourage a sense of pride in the company.

By recognizing individual contributions, you can foster a positive company culture and motivate and engage your employees. This can help improve your company culture and allow to reach its full potential.

6. Support employee empowerment

Supporting employee empowerment is an important step in the process of improving your company culture and allowing it to reach its full potential.

By empowering your employees, you can give them the autonomy and support they need to take ownership of their work and make decisions. This can help foster a sense of ownership and accountability among your employees and contribute to a positive company culture.

Here are some steps you can take to support employee empowerment:

Provide training and development opportunities: Provide your employees with training and development opportunities to help them grow and develop their skills.

Encourage decision-making: Encourage your employees to make decisions and take ownership of their work.

Provide support and resources: Provide your employees with the support and resources they need to succeed in their roles.

Foster open communication: Encourage open and honest communication between employees and management to help create a collaborative and supportive environment.

Delegate responsibility: Delegate responsibility and give your employees the autonomy they need to take ownership of their work. By supporting employee empowerment, you can create a culture that encourages collaboration, innovation, and success. This, in turn, can help improve your company culture and allow it to reach its full potential

A strong company culture is more than just a buzzword. It is the foundation of a thriving and successful organization. It not only attracts top talent but also fosters engagement, motivation, and long-term commitment among employees. When employees feel valued and connected to their workplace, they are more likely to be productive, innovative, and dedicated to the company's mission. A positive culture promotes trust, collaboration, and a sense of purpose, all of which contribute to a healthier work environment and better business outcomes.

However, cultivating a great company culture requires more than just well-defined values. It demands intentional leadership, consistent effort, and a genuine investment in employee well-being.

Organizations that prioritize culture create teams that are resilient, adaptable, and motivated to drive long-term success. A thriving workplace culture doesn't just boost morale; it enhances job satisfaction, improves retention rates, and strengthens the overall brand reputation. Employees who feel supported and empowered are more likely to contribute their best work, leading to increased efficiency and stronger business performance.

The six steps provide a practical framework for strengthening workplace culture. By focusing on one or two key initiatives and gradually implementing more, companies can create meaningful and lasting improvements. Small, intentional changes such as fostering open communication, recognizing employee achievements, and promoting a healthy work-life balance, can have a profound impact over time.

A strong company culture isn't built overnight. It requires time, dedication, and a continuous commitment to improvement. However, when nurtured properly, it can transform an organization into a place where employees feel inspired, motivated, and deeply connected to their work. A positive culture fosters collaboration, innovation, and a

shared sense of purpose, creating an environment where both individuals and the company as a whole can thrive.

Ultimately, a well-crafted company culture isn't just an advantage; it's a fundamental pillar of sustainable success and long-term growth. Businesses that prioritize their culture will not only attract and retain top talent but also build resilient teams that can adapt to challenges and drive innovation. In a rapidly evolving professional landscape, a strong workplace culture serves as a guiding force, shaping the company's future and ensuring continued success for years to come.

MICROCASTING

Supercharge Your Business!

Do you want to find new ways to add additional income to your coaching, consulting, or content creation business?

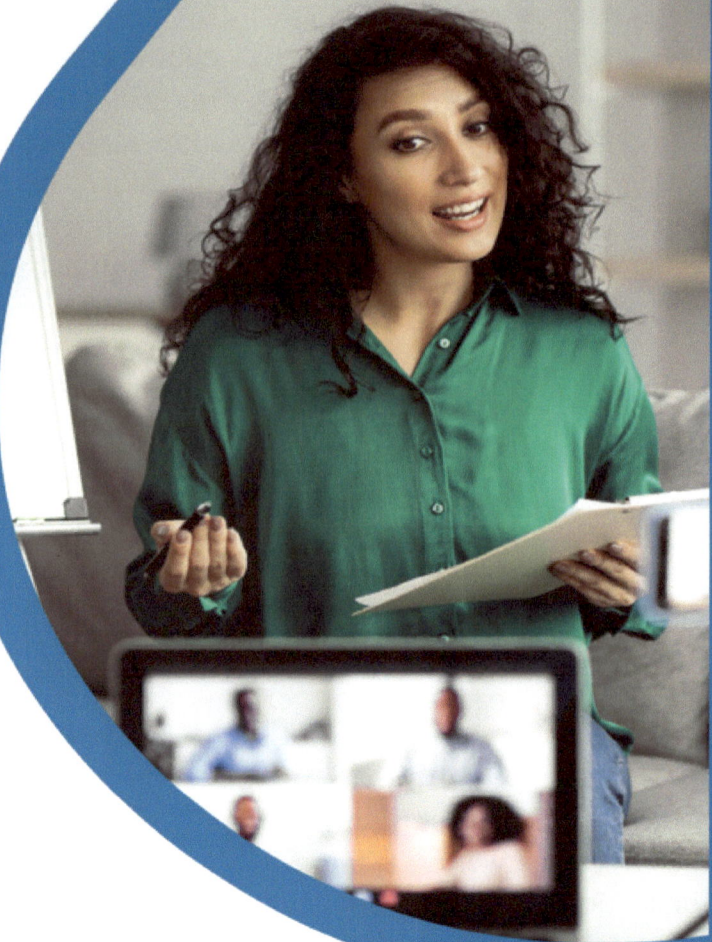

eLearning Portals by Microcasting is specifically designed for Coaches, Consultants, and Course Creators to engage your customers, establish yourself as a thought leader, and grow your revenues.

Here are just a few things you can do with **Microcasting**:

- ⊘ **Start selling** your courses and programs.
- ⊘ Create a **paid membership site** to grow your revenues.
- ⊘ Build a free membership site to **increase lead gen**.
- ⊘ Easily **integrate eLearning** into your marketing website.
- ⊘ Create **individualized customer portals** .
- ⊘ And so much more...

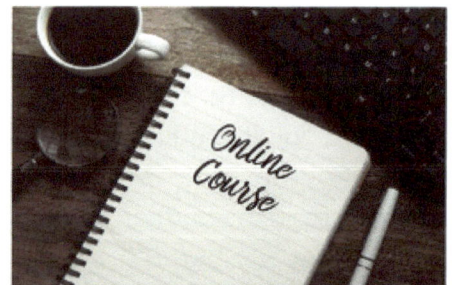

Microcasting is an all-in-one online learning platform that makes it easy for course creators to design, manage, and market their courses. With its personalized eLearning experience, you can keep your current customers engaged with your business, generating more upsells and higher renewal rates. Create courses quickly and effortlessly - all with the help of Microcasting!

Try Microcasting today and start transforming your business!

Request a demo - email us at ✉ info@microcasting.com **OR VISIT** ⊕ www.elearning-portals.com

The Importance of Self-Improvement for Success: 5 Ways to Work on Yourself

Self-improvement is a journey of personal growth that involves enhancing your skills , knowledge, and abilities in order to become the best version of yourself. It's an ongoing process that requires effort, dedication, and a willingness to learn and adapt. But why is self-improvement so important

The Importance of Self-Improvement for Success:

Self-improvement is essential for success in both your personal and professional life. When you work on yourself and strive to become the best version of yourself, you'll be more confident, capable, and competent in everything you do. This can help you achieve your goals and reach your full potential in your career and other areas of your life.

So, if you want to achieve success in your life, don't underestimate the power of self-improvement. Take the time to work on yourself and strive for personal growth, and you'll be well on your way to achieving your goals and reaching your full potential.

Here are five ways that self-improvement can lead to success:

Self-improvement is a journey of personal growth that involves enhancing your skills, knowledge, and abilities in order to become the best version of yourself. It's an ongoing process that requires effort, dedication, and a willingness to learn and adapt. But why is self-improvement so important?

Five ways that self-improvement can lead to success:

Improved communication and interpersonal skills: Effective communication is crucial in any situation, whether you're giving a presentation at work or simply having a conversation with a friend. By working on your communication skills, you'll be able to express your thoughts and ideas, as well as listen more effectively to others. This can lead to better relationships, more successful collaborations, and greater overall success.

Enhanced decision-making and problem-solving abilities: The ability to make good decisions and solve problems is essential for success in any field. By continuously learning and improving your critical thinking skills, you'll be better equipped to make informed decisions and find creative solutions to challenges that come your way.

Increased confidence and self-esteem: When you work on yourself and make progress in your personal growth, you'll naturally become more confident in your abilities. This increased self-confidence can translate into a greater sense of self-worth and improved self-

esteem. This can help you feel more capable and capable of tackling new challenges and opportunities, leading to greater success.

Staying up-to-date with industry trends and developments: In today's fast-paced world, it's important to stay current with the latest trends and developments in your industry. By continuously learning and improving your skills, you'll be better equipped to adapt to change and take advantage of new opportunities as they arise.

Improved time management and productivity: When you work on yourself and become more organized and efficient, you'll naturally be more productive. By setting goals, prioritizing tasks, and finding ways to streamline your workflow, you'll be able to get more done in less time. This can lead to greater success in your personal and professional endeavors.

Self-improvement is an essential component of success in both your personal and professional life. By working on yourself and striving for personal growth, you'll be more confident, capable, and competent in everything you do. So don't underestimate the power of self-improvement – start working on yourself today, and watch your success soar!

Identifying areas for self-improvement

Identifying areas for self-improvement is an important first step in the self-improvement process. It's important to identify specific areas where you want to improve and focus your efforts on making progress in these areas. But how do you go about identifying areas for self-improvement?

Here are a few tips:

Reflect on your strengths and weaknesses: One of the best ways to identify areas for self-improvement is to take some time to reflect on your strengths and weaknesses. Think about your skills, knowledge, and abilities, and consider where you excel and where you may need to improve. This can help you focus your efforts on the areas where you have the most potential for growth.

Seek feedback from others: Another effective way to identify areas for self-improvement is to seek feedback from others. Ask trusted colleagues, friends, or family members for their honest opinions and insights on your strengths and areas for growth. This can provide valuable perspective and help you identify areas where you may need to focus your efforts.

Set goals for personal growth: Setting specific, measurable, attainable, relevant, and time-bound (SMART) goals can be an effective way to identify areas for self-improvement. Consider what you want to achieve in your personal and professional life, and set goals to help guide your self-improvement journey.

By taking the time to reflect on your strengths and weaknesses, seeking feedback from others, and setting goals for personal growth, you can identify specific areas for self-improvement and focus your efforts on making progress in these areas.

The role of learning in self-improvement:

Learning is an essential part of the self-improvement process. It's important to continuously seek out new knowledge and skills in order to grow and improve as a person.

Education and training programs : One way to learn and improve your skills is to participate in education and training programs. These programs can range from formal degree programs to short courses or workshops. By enrolling in a program, you'll have the opportunity to learn from experts in your field and gain valuable knowledge and skills that can help you grow and succeed.

Online courses: In today's digital age, there are numerous online courses and resources available for learning new skills and knowledge. These courses can be a convenient and flexible way to learn, and many offer certification or other forms of recognition upon completion.

Workshops and seminars: Attending workshops and seminars can also be a great way to learn and improve your skills. These events often feature presentations or lectures by industry experts and can provide valuable insights and knowledge that you can apply to your personal or professional life.

Stay up-to-date with industry trends and developments: In addition to formal learning opportunities, it's important to stay up-to-date with the latest trends and developments in your industry.

The role of self-discipline in self-improvement:

Self-discipline is a crucial aspect of the self-improvement process. It's what allows you to stay focused and motivated, and take consistent action towards your goals. Without self-discipline, it can be easy to become sidetracked or lose sight of your priorities.

Here are a few ways that self-discipline can support your self-improvement journey:

Setting and sticking to boundaries: One aspect of self-discipline is setting boundaries for yourself and sticking to them. This could include setting limits on social media or screen time, setting aside dedicated time for self-improvement, or saying no to distracting or unimportant tasks. By setting and respecting boundaries, you'll be better able to stay focused and achieve your goals.

Forming healthy habits: Another way that self-discipline can support your self-improvement journey is by helping you form healthy habits. Whether it's exercising regularly, eating a nutritious diet, or making time for daily meditation, self-discipline can help you stick to healthy habits that will support your overall well-being and personal growth.

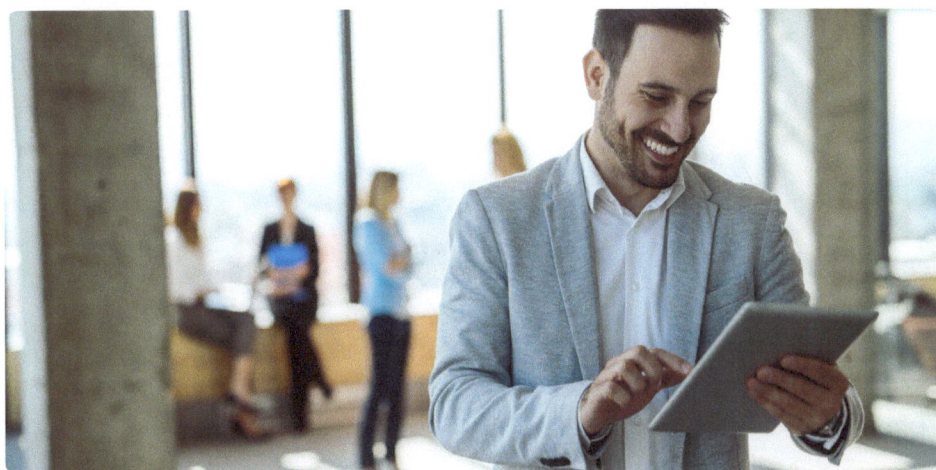

Staying motivated and focused: Self-discipline can also help you stay motivated and focused as you work towards your goals. By setting clear objectives and consistently taking small steps towards them, you'll be able to stay motivated and on track.

In summary, self-discipline is a key component of the self-improvement process. By setting boundaries, forming healthy habits, and staying motivated and focused, you can take consistent action towards your goals and achieve success in your personal and professional endeavour

Practical ways to work on yourself:

So, you've identified areas for self-improvement and are ready to start working on yourself. But where do you begin?

Here are five practical tips to help you get started:

Set aside dedicated time for self-improvement: To make progress in your personal growth, you'll need to set aside dedicated time to focus on your goals and priorities. This could be a few hours each week, or even a few minutes each day. Whatever works best for you, make sure to carve out dedicated time to work on yourself and make progress.

Seek guidance and support from mentors and coaches : Another effective way to work on yourself is to seek guidance and support from mentors and coaches.

These individuals can provide valuable insights, advice, and encouragement as you navigate the self-improvement process.

Stay motivated and accountable through self-reflection and self-assessment: It's important to stay motivated and accountable as you work on yourself. One way to do this is to regularly reflect on your progress and assess your strengths and areas for improvement. This can help you stay focused and motivated, and make sure you're making progress towards your goals.

Find ways to challenge yourself: To make real progress in your personal growth, you'll need to step outside of your comfort zone and challenge yourself. This could mean taking on new responsibilities at work, trying something new, or even learning a new skill. By pushing yourself and taking on new challenges, you'll be able to grow and improve in ways you may not have thought possible.

Surround yourself with positive and supportive individuals: Finally, it's important to surround yourself with positive and supportive individuals who will encourage and support you on your self-improvement journey.

These could be friends, family members, colleagues, or mentors. These individuals can provide valuable guidance, motivation, and encouragement as you work towards your goals.

By following these practical tips and making self-improvement a priority, you can work on yourself and achieve your full potential.

Conclusion:

In conclusion, self-improvement is an essential component of success in both your personal and professional life. By identifying areas for improvement, seeking new knowledge and skills, and staying motivated and accountable, you can work on yourself and achieve your full potential. So don't be afraid to take the first step on your self-improvement journey – you never know what amazing things you may accomplish!

Remember, self-improvement is an ongoing process that requires effort, dedication, and a willingness to learn and adapt. By committing to personal growth and development, you can become the best version of yourself and achieve success in all areas of your life.

The Role of Emotional Intelligence in Business Success

Emotional intelligence (EI) is a hot topic in today's business world. It's the ability to understand and manage our own emotions, as well as the emotions of others. It's the key to success in any field, but especially in business. The ability to read a room, understand the emotions of clients and colleagues, and respond appropriately can make or break a deal, a project, or a career. The good news is that EI is a set of skills that can be learned and developed over time.

In this article, we will explore the concept of emotional intelligence and its importance in the business world. We will also delve into the different components of EI and how they contribute to overall effectiveness. We will examine the impact of EI on business success and discuss ways to develop emotional intelligence in the workplace. By the end of this post, you will have a better understanding of how emotional intelligence can help you succeed in business and how to start developing your own emotional intelligence skills.

Understanding Emotional Intelligence

Emotional intelligence is the ability to understand and manage our own emotions, as well as the emotions of others. It's a combination of cognitive and emotional abilities that allow us to navigate social situations with ease and effectiveness.

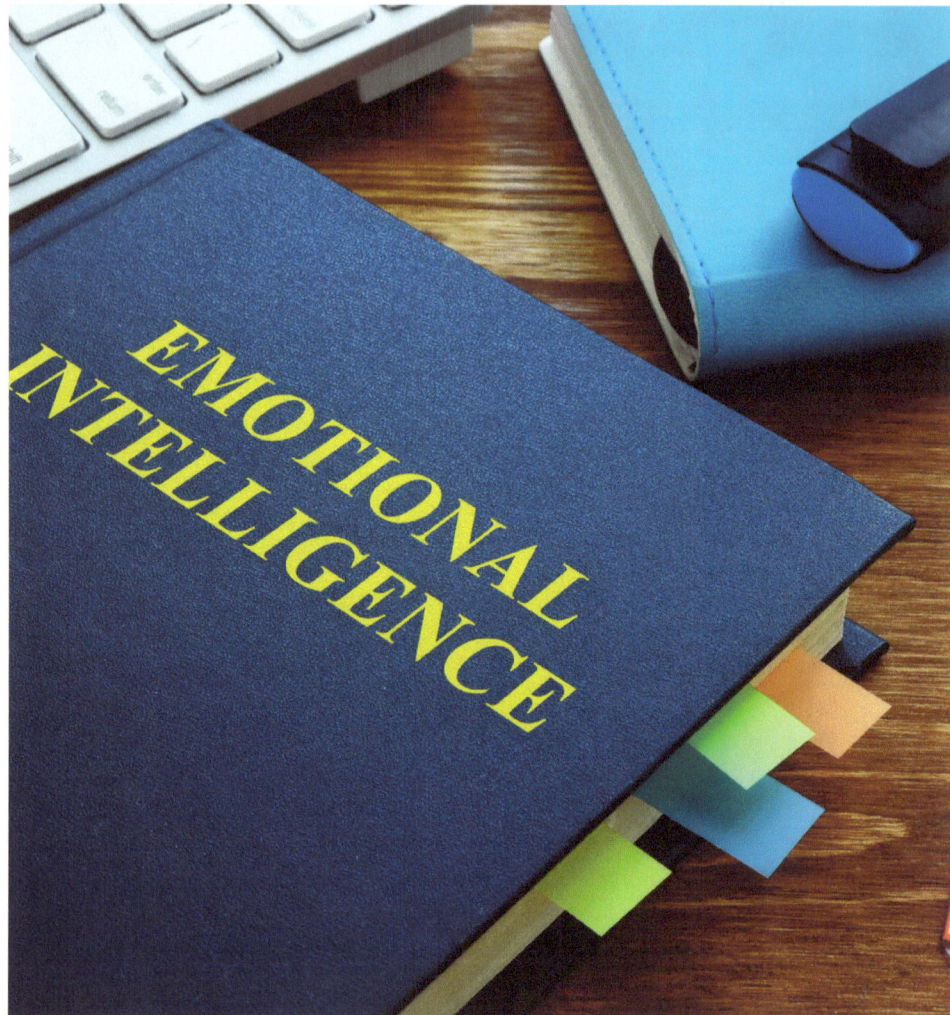

There are several key components of emotional intelligence that contribute to overall effectiveness. These include:

Self-awareness: The ability to recognize and understand our own emotions, as well as how they influence our thoughts, behaviors, and decisions. This includes being aware of our strengths and weaknesses, as well as how we respond to different situations.

Motivation: The drive to achieve our goals and aspirations, as well as the ability to stay motivated and engaged in the face of obstacles. This includes being able to set and work towards personal and and professional goals.

Empathy: The ability to understand and share the feelings of others. This includes being able to read the emotions of others and respond appropriately.

Social skills: The ability to build and maintain positive relationships with others. This includes being able to communicate effectively, resolve conflicts, and influence others.

All these components interact and contribute to overall emotional intelligence. For example, high self-awareness is necessary for effective self-regulation, and a lack of empathy can hinder social skills. It is also important to note that emotional intelligence can be developed and improved over time, with the right training and practice.

Emotional intelligence plays a critical role in personal and professional development. It can help us build stronger relationships, communicate more effectively, and make better decisions. It is also becoming increasingly important in the business world, as companies seek to create a positive and productive corporate culture. Emotionally intelligent leaders are able to create a positive work environment, foster collaboration, and inspire their teams to achieve great results.

In short, understanding emotional intelligence is crucial for personal and professional development. It is the key to success in any field, but especially in business. By understanding the different components of EI, we can start to develop our own emotional intelligence skills and become more effective in our personal and professional lives.

In short, understanding emotional intelligence is crucial for personal and professional development. It is the key to success in any field, but especially in business. By understanding the different components of EI, we can start to develop our own emotional intelligence skills and become more effective in our personal and professional lives.

The Impact of Emotional Intelligence on Business Success

Emotional intelligence plays a critical role in business success. The ability to understand and manage our own emotions, as well as the emotions of others, can greatly impact how we communicate, lead, and make

decisions in the workplace. Here are some of the ways that emotional intelligence can contribute to business success:

1. Improved Communication and Teamwork: Emotionally intelligent individuals are able to communicate effectively and build strong relationships with their colleagues. They can also understand the emotions of others and respond appropriately. This leads to better teamwork, collaboration and a more positive work environment.

2. Stronger Leadership: Emotionally intelligent leaders are able to read the emotions of their team members and respond in a way that is supportive and motivating. They can also communicate effectively and inspire their team to achieve great results.

3. Better Decision-Making and Problem-Solving: Emotionally intelligent individuals are able to recognize and understand their own emotions, which can help them make better decisions and solve problems more effectively. They are also able to read the emotions of others, which can provide valuable insight into a situation.

4. Improved Relationships with Customers and Clients: Emotionally intelligent individuals are able to understand the emotions of customers and clients and respond appropriately.

This leads to better customer service and stronger relationships with clients.

In conclusion, emotional intelligence plays a vital role in business success. It can improve communication and teamwork, enhance leadership skills, aid decision making and problem solving, improve relationships with customers and clients and create a positive corporate culture. By understanding and developing emotional intelligence, businesses and individuals can achieve great results and excel in their field.

Developing Emotional Intelligence in the Workplace

As we have discussed, emotional intelligence is a set of skills that can be learned and developed over time. In order to be successful in the workplace, it is important for individuals and companies to invest in emotional intelligence development. Here are some ways to develop emotional intelligence in the workplace:

Training: One of the most effective ways to develop emotional intelligence is through training . This can include workshops, seminars, and classes that focus on different components of emotional intelligence, such as self-awareness, self-regulation, motivation, empathy, and social skills. These training sessions

can be led by experts in the field, and can provide employees with valuable tools and strategies for developing their emotional intelligence skills.

Mentoring: Another effective way to develop emotional intelligence is through mentoring. This can involve pairing more experienced employees with less experienced employees, in order to provide guidance and support. A mentor can provide feedback, advice, and support as an employee develops their emotional intelligence skills.

Coaching: Similar to mentoring, coaching can be an effective way to develop emotional intelligence. A coach can work one-on-one with an employee, providing them with feedback, guidance, and support as they develop their emotional intelligence skills.

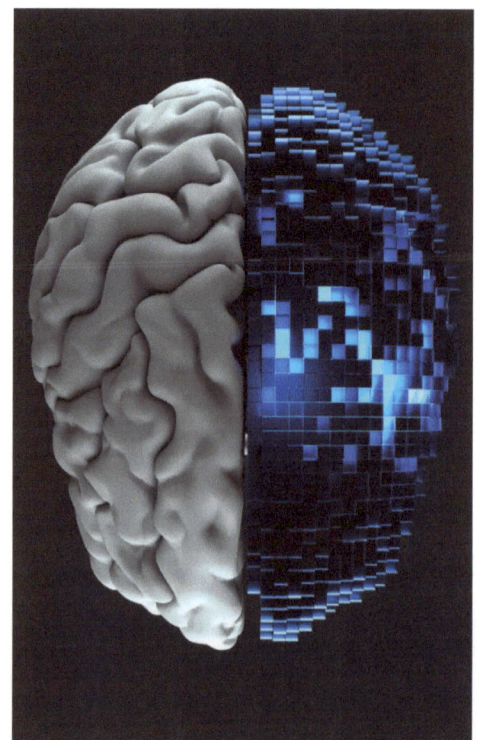

Supportive Environment: Companies can create a supportive environment for emotional intelligence development by providing employees with the resources they need to develop their skills. This can include things like access to training and development opportunities, as well as a positive and supportive work culture.

Technology: With the rise of AI and machine learning technology, companies are now able to provide employees with virtual emotional intelligence training. This technology can provide employees with personalized feedback and guidance, as well as interactive exercises and simulations to help them develop their emotional intelligence skills.

By providing employees with the tools and resources they need to develop their emotional intelligence skills, companies can create a more positive and productive work environment. When employees are emotionally intelligent, they are more likely to communicate effectively, lead effectively, and make better decisions. This can lead to greater success for both the individual and the company.

In conclusion, developing emotional intelligence in the workplace is crucial for both personal and professional development. By providing training, mentoring, coaching and creating a supportive environment, as well as utilizing technology, companies can help employees develop their emotional intelligence skills, leading to a more positive and productive work environment and better business results.

Real-world Examples of Emotional Intelligence in Business Success

As we have discussed, emotional intelligence plays a critical role in business success. But how exactly can it be applied in the real world? Here are a few examples of how emotional intelligence has been used to achieve success in the business world:

A leader with high emotional intelligence was able to turn around a struggling team within a company. By understanding and managing the emotions of her team members, she was able to create a more positive and productive work environment, leading to improved performance and greater success for the team.

A salesperson with strong empathy was able to close more deals with clients by understanding their needs and emotions. By being able to read the emotions of her clients, she was able to tailor her sales pitch to meet their specific needs, leading to more successful sales.

A company with a positive corporate culture, fostered by emotionally intelligent leaders, was able to attract and retain top talent. By creating a supportive and motivating work environment, the company was

able to attract the best and brightest employees, which in turn helped the company to grow and excel

These examples demonstrate the tangible benefits of emotional intelligence in the business world. They show how emotional intelligence can be used to improve communication, teamwork, and leadership, as well as to create a positive and productive work environment. By understanding the principles of emotional intelligence and seeing how they have been applied in the real world, readers can be inspired to apply the same principles in their own careers.

As we have seen, emotional intelligence plays a critical role in business success. By understanding the different components of emotional intelligence, the impact it has on business success, and ways to develop emotional intelligence in the workplace, and now, by seeing the real-world examples of its application, readers will be better equipped to apply the principles of emotional intelligence in their own lives and careers.

Conclusion

In conclusion, emotional intelligence plays a critical role in business success. The ability to understand and manage our own emotions, as well as the emotions of others, can greatly impact how we communicate, lead, and make decisions in the workplace. We have discussed the different components of emotional intelligence and how they contribute to overall effectiveness, the impact of emotional intelligence on business success, and ways to develop emotional intelligence in the workplace.

We have seen that emotional intelligence can improve communication and teamwork, enhance leadership skills, aid decision-making and problem-solving, improve relationships with customers and clients, and create a positive corporate culture. Companies that invest in emotional intelligence development can create a more positive and productive work environment, leading to greater success for both the individual and the company.

Emotional intelligence (EI) is a skill that can be developed over time, with key aspects like self-awareness, empathy, and communication driving personal and professional success. In the workplace, strong EI enhances leadership, teamwork, and decision-making, fostering better relationships and productivity.

Leaders and employees with high EI navigate challenges, resolve conflicts, and collaborate effectively, contributing to long-term business success.

Recognizing EI's value is just the start and actively developing it drives real growth. Through self-reflection, mindfulness, and empathy, individuals improve emotional management and connections.

Organizations that invest in EI training foster stronger teams, better customer interactions, and adaptability. Prioritizing EI enhances workplace performance and enriches personal relationships, promoting overall well-being.

FROGMAN MINDFULNESS

Jon Macaskill
US Navy SEAL Commander (Ret)
Keynote Speaking
One on One Coaching
Mindfulness Teaching
www.frogmanmindfulness.com
757-619-1211

Effective Strategies for Managing a Remote Team

In today's fast-paced business environment, more and more companies are turning to remote work as a way to increase productivity, reduce costs, and attract top talent . While remote work offers many benefits, it also presents its own set of challenges, particularly when it comes to managing a remote team.

Managing a remote team requires a different approach than managing a traditional, in-office team. Communication, trust, and employee engagement are all critical factors in ensuring the success of a remote team. In this article, we will explore effective strategies for managing a remote team, including tips for clear and frequent communication, building trust and accountability, and promoting employee engagement and motivation. We will also discuss how to maintain company culture, manage remote team dynamics and increase productivity.

As remote work becomes more prevalent, it's essential for managers to understand how to effectively lead and manage remote teams. In this article, we'll provide insights and strategies to help managers navigate the unique challenges of remote work and lead a successful remote team.

Onboarding and Training

Onboarding and training are crucial strategies for managing a remote team. These strategies help new hires understand their roles and responsibilities and become productive members of the team as quickly as possible. A comprehensive onboarding program is essential for remote teams. This program should include all the information and resources that new hires need to get up to speed, such as company policies and procedures, job descriptions, and training materials. Regular check-ins and feedback sessions can ensure that new hires are on track and understand their roles and responsibilities.

Remote teams also benefit from using technology to facilitate communication and collaboration. Video conferencing and screen sharing tools enable remote team members to share information and collaborate on projects easily. Project management and collaboration software can keep remote teams organized and on track.

Creating a sense of community among remote team members is also important. Regular team meetings, both virtual and in-person, and encouraging regular communication among team members can foster a sense of community. Internal social media platforms or company chat channels can provide a platform for team members to connect and communicate with each other.

Finally, regular feedback and recognition is key to maintaining a positive and productive remote team. Providing feedback on performance, progress, and goals can help remote team members stay motivated and engaged. Recognizing and rewarding team members for their hard work and accomplishments can boost morale and foster a positive work environment.

Overall, onboarding and training are essential strategies for managing a remote team.

By implementing a comprehensive onboarding program, utilizing technology, fostering a sense of community, and providing regular feedback and recognition, managers can ensure that new hires are properly onboarded and trained and that the entire team is productive and engaged.

Time Management

Time management is a critical strategy for successfully managing a remote team. With team members working from different locations and time zones, it can be challenging to coordinate schedules and ensure that everyone is on the same page. However, with the right time management strategies in place, it is possible to keep remote teams productive and on track.

One important strategy for successfully managing remote teams is to establish clear

expectations and deadlines for tasks and projects. This helps team members understand what is expected of them and when things need to be done, which can prevent confusion and delays. By setting clear deadlines, team members will be more motivated to work efficiently and effectively.

Another key strategy for successfully managing remote teams is to use project management software to stay organized and on track. These tools allow team members to see what tasks they need to complete and when they need to complete them, which can help keep everyone accountable and focused. Additionally, by using time tracking software, managers can monitor and optimize team member's working hours.

Another strategy is to schedule regular team meetings, both virtual and in-person, and encourage team members to communicate regularly. This can help team members stay connected and informed about what is happening in the team, and ensure that everyone is on the same page. Additionally, creating a shared calendar that everyone can access can help to ensure that everyone is aware of important deadlines and schedule conflicts.

Finally, Encourage team members to work flexible hours if possible, and accommodate different time zones. This can help to ensure that everyone is able to work during their most productive hours and can prevent burnout.

Communication

Effective communication is one of the most important strategies for managing a remote team. When team members are working from different locations and time zones, it can be challenging to stay connected and ensure that everyone is on the same page. However, with the right communication strategies in place, it is possible to keep remote teams productive and on track.

One key strategy for managing remote teams is to establish clear lines of communication. This includes setting up regular team meetings, both virtual and in-person, and encouraging team members to communicate regularly. This can help team members stay connected and informed about what is happening in the team, and ensure that everyone is on the same page. Additionally, creating a shared calendar that everyone can access can help to ensure that everyone is aware of important deadlines and schedule conflicts.

Another important strategy for managing remote teams is to use technology to facilitate communication and collaboration. Video conferencing and screen sharing tools enable remote team members to share information and collaborate on projects easily. Project management and collaboration software can keep remote teams organized and on track. Additionally, messaging and instant messaging tools can be used to quickly communicate and resolve any issues or concerns.

Another key strategy is to establish clear communication protocols and guidelines. This includes outlining how and when team members should communicate, as well as what type of information should be shared. This can help to ensure that everyone is on the same page and that communication is effective and efficient.

Finally, it's important to actively listen and encourage feedback. Managers should make an effort to actively listen to team members and encourage feedback, this can help to identify any issues or concerns and address them quickly. Additionally, regular performance reviews can help to identify any communication-related issues and address them.

In conclusion, effective communication is one of the most important strategies for managing a remote team. By establishing clear lines of communication, utilizing technology, establishing clear communication protocols, and actively listening and encouraging feedback, managers can keep remote teams productive and on track.

Trust and accountability

Managing a remote team can be challenging, especially when it comes to building trust and ensuring accountability among team members. However, with the right strategies in place, it is possible to foster a productive and collaborative remote team environment.

One essential strategy for building trust is clear communication and setting expectations. This includes outlining roles and responsibilities, setting clear deadlines and goals, and providing regular updates and progress reports. This can help team members understand what is expected of them, and prevent confusion and delays. Clear communication also helps team members to feel more

connected and engaged with the team.

Another important strategy is to use technology to facilitate communication and collaboration. Video conferencing, screen sharing, and project management software are essential tools for remote teams. These tools allow team members to share information, collaborate on projects, and stay organized, which helps to build trust and collaboration among team members.

Accountability is also crucial in managing a remote team. One way to ensure accountability is by setting clear performance metrics and regular check-ins. By monitoring progress and providing regular feedback, managers can ensure that team members are meeting their goals and responsibilities, and address any issues that may arise. Additionally, creating a culture of transparency and open communication can help to ensure that team members take ownership of their work and are held accountable for their actions.

Finally, recognizing and rewarding team members for their hard work and accomplishments can help build trust and foster a positive work environment. This not only helps to build trust but also motivates team members to be accountable and take ownership of their work.

Employee Wellness

Employee wellness is an important aspect of managing a remote team. As more and more companies are transitioning to a remote work environment, it's important to ensure that employees are not only productive, but also happy and healthy.

One way to promote employee wellness is to encourage regular breaks throughout the day. Sitting in front of a computer for long periods of time can lead to eye strain, back pain, and other physical problems. Encourage your team to take short breaks throughout the day to stretch, move around, and recharge.

Another way to promote employee wellness is to encourage healthy habits such as regular exercise and healthy eating. Many remote workers fall into the trap of snacking on junk food and not getting enough physical activity. Encourage your team to eat healthy and stay active by offering suggestions for healthy meals, providing a fitness allowance, or even hosting virtual fitness classes.

It's also important to address the emotional and mental well-being of your team. Remote work can be isolating and can lead to feelings of loneliness and anxiety.

Encourage team members to connect with each other through virtual team building activities or by setting up regular video meetings.

Lastly, the company should provide access to mental health resources to support

the employee's emotional and mental well-being. It is crucial to have a safe and confidential space where employees can talk to a professional.

In conclusion, promoting employee wellness is an important strategy for managing a remote team. By encouraging regular breaks, healthy habits, social interaction, and providing mental health resources, you can help your team stay happy, healthy, and productive.

Collaboration and Productivity

Collaboration and productivity are two key strategies for managing a remote team. As more and more companies are transitioning to a remote work environment, it's important to ensure that employees are able to work together effectively and efficiently.

One way to promote collaboration is to use a project management tool such as Asana, Trello, or Monday.com. These tools allow team members to easily share and access information, track progress, and communicate with one another. This can help to ensure that everyone is on the same page and that tasks are completed on time.

Another way to promote collaboration is to use video conferencing tools such as Zoom, Google Meet, or Skype. Video conferencing allows team members to see and hear one another, which can help to build stronger connections and improve communication. This can be especially useful when working on a team project or when making important decisions.

To promote productivity, it's important to set clear goals and expectations for your team. Clearly defined goals and deadlines can help to ensure that everyone is working towards the same objective and that tasks are completed on time. It's also important to provide your team with the resources and support they need to be successful.

Additionally, it's important to establish clear communication guidelines and protocols. This can include setting regular check-ins, establishing specific communication channels for certain types of conversations, and encouraging open and honest feedback.

Collaboration and productivity are two important strategies for managing a remote team. By using project management and video conferencing tools, setting clear goals and expectations, providing resources and support, and establishing clear communication guidelines, you can help your team work effectively and efficiently.

Managing a remote team comes with its own set of challenges, but with the right strategies in place, it can be a success. One of the key strategies is to promote employee wellness by encouraging regular breaks, healthy habits, social interaction, and providing mental health resources.

Another key strategy is to promote collaboration and productivity by using project management and video conferencing tools, setting clear goals and expectations, providing resources and support, and establishing clear communication guidelines.

Additionally, building trust and fostering open communication within your team is essential for a strong remote work environment. Encouraging transparency, active collaboration, and regular check-ins can help bridge the gap created by physical distance. Providing opportunities for professional development, such as training sessions, mentorship programs, and skill-building workshops, ensures that employees continue to grow and stay engaged. By implementing these strategies, you can create a cohesive, motivated, and high-performing remote team that works efficiently and achieves long-term success.